R-3139-NIE

# Teacher Evaluation

## A Study of Effective Practices

Arthur E. Wise, Linda Darling-Hammond,
Milbrey W. McLaughlin, Harriet T. Bernstein

June 1984

Prepared for the
National Institute of Education

REF
LB
2838
.T39
1984

R0034/6859

# PREFACE

This report describes a 1983 Rand study of teacher evaluation practices. The study was financed by the National Institute of Education, which correctly predicted the growing interest in improving teacher evaluation. The report should be of interest to those initiating or revising teacher evaluation procedures.

School systems evaluate teachers to facilitate decisions about teacher status and to help teachers improve their performance. Most existing literature on teacher evaluation concerns evaluation instruments and ways to improve the technical reliability and validity of such instruments (that is, how consistently and how accurately they measure teaching performance).[1]

The present study focused on the actual operation of teacher evaluation procedures in school systems. It examined not only the instruments and procedures, but also the implementation processes and the organizational contexts within which they operate. This approach enabled the authors to observe whether and how teacher evaluation results are used by the organization. It also indicated the broader organizational conditions needed to initiate and sustain effective teacher evaluation practices.

A panel composed of representatives of education and education-related organizations advised the study. The panel included:

Dr. Gordon Cawelti, Executive Director, Association for Supervision and Curriculum Development

Dr. Susan S. Ellis, Teacher Leader for Staff Development, Greenwich (Connecticut) Public Schools (representing the National Staff Development Council)

Ms. Anita Epstein, Governmental Affairs Director, National Association of State Boards of Education

Dr. Jeremiah Floyd, Associate Executive Director, Office of Communications and Membership Relations, National School Boards Association

Dr. David G. Imig, Executive Director, American Association of Colleges for Teacher Education

---

[1]See Linda Darling-Hammond, Arthur E. Wise, and Sara R. Pease, "Teacher Evaluation in the Organizational Context: A Review of the Literature," *Review of Educational Research*, Fall 1983.

Dr. James Keefe, Director of Research, National Association of Secondary School Principals

Ms. Lucille Maurer, Member, Maryland House of Delegates (representing the National Conference of State Legislatures)

Dr. Bernard McKenna, Program Development Specialist, National Education Association

Ms. Margaret Montgomery, Professional Development Specialist, National Association of Elementary School Principals

Dr. Reuben Pierce, Acting Assistant Superintendent for Quality Assurance, District of Columbia Public Schools

Dr. William Pierce, Executive Director, Council of Chief State School Officers

Ms. Marilyn Rauth, Director, Educational Issues Department, American Federation of Teachers

Dr. Robert W. Peebles, Superintendent of Schools, Alexandria (Virginia) City Public Schools (representing the American Association of School Administrators).

The involvement of the panel was meant to encourage a study and report that would be relevant to groups with a stake in teacher evaluation. The panel advised on the research plan, helped to identify school districts with highly developed teacher evaluation procedures, and commented on drafts of the report. The participation of these panel members, however, does not necessarily imply their endorsement of the report's conclusions.

The panel advised that the report be kept short so that it would be widely read. Following this advice, the authors present in this volume only their findings, analyses, conclusions, and recommendations. The four case studies that provided most of the data for the report are summarized here; they are also being published separately as *Case Studies for Teacher Evaluation: A Study of Effective Practices*, N-2133-NIE, June 1984.

# SUMMARY

The new concern for the quality of education and of teachers is being translated into merit-pay, career-ladder, and master-teacher policies that presuppose the existence of effective teacher evaluation systems. As a result, many school districts will be reassessing their teacher evaluation practices.

School district administrators must understand the educational and organizational implications of the teacher evaluation system that they adopt, because that system can define the nature of teaching and education in their schools. In particular, the system can either reinforce the idea of teaching as a profession, or it can further deprofessionalize teaching, making it less able to attract and retain talented teachers.

## FRAMEWORK OF TEACHER EVALUATION

Teacher evaluation may serve four basic purposes: individual staff development, school improvement, individual personnel decisions, and school status decisions. The first two purposes involve improvement; the second two, accountability. Although many teacher evaluation systems may seek to accomplish all four of these purposes, different processes and methods may better suit individual objectives. In particular, improvement and accountability require different standards of adequacy and evidence.

For purposes of accountability, teacher evaluation processes must be capable of yielding fairly objective, standardized, and externally defensible information about teacher performance. For improvement objectives, evaluation processes must yield descriptive information that illuminates sources of difficulty, as well as viable courses for change.

To improve a teacher's performance, the school system must enlist the teacher's cooperation, motivate him (or her), and guide him through the steps to improvement. For the individual, improvement relies on the development of two important conditions: the knowledge that a course of action is the correct one and a sense of empowerment or efficacy, that is, a perception that pursuing a given course of action is both worthwhile and possible.

The implementation of any school policy, including a teacher evaluation policy, represents a continuous interplay among diverse policy goals, established rules and procedures (concerning both the policy in question and other aspects of the school's operation), intergroup bargaining and value choices, and the local institutional context. The political climate of the school system, the relationship of the teachers' organization to district management, the nature of other educational policies and operating programs in the district, and the size and structure of the system and its bureaucracy all influence teacher evaluation procedures.

## SURVEY OF EVALUATION PRACTICES IN 32 SCHOOL DISTRICTS

We undertook this study to find teacher evaluation processes that produce information that school districts can use for helping teachers to improve and/or for making personnel decisions. The study began with a review of the literature and a preliminary survey of 32 districts identified as having highly developed teacher evaluation systems.

Teacher evaluation practices differed substantially in the 32 school districts. Although the practices seemed similar in broad outline, they diverged as local implementation choices were made. Our preliminary assessment led us to conclude that school authorities do not agree on what constitutes the best practice with regard to instrumentation, frequency of evaluation, the role of the teacher in the process, or how the information could or should inform other district activities. These differences in practices, we believe, indicate that teacher evaluation presently is an underconceptualized and underdeveloped activity.

Despite differences in level of development and diversity of local implementation choices, the major problems associated with teacher evaluation practices were similar in the 32 districts surveyed. Almost all survey respondents felt that principals lacked sufficient resolve and competence to evaluate accurately. Other problems included teacher resistance or apathy, the lack of uniformity and consistency of evaluation within a school system, inadequate training for evaluators, and shortcomings in the evaluation of secondary school staff and specialists.

Respondents consistently reported two positive results of teacher evaluation: improved teacher-administrator communication and increased teacher awareness of instructional goals and classroom practices. In most of the 32 districts, the teacher evaluation system has led to personnel actions. Although few districts used evaluation outcomes to terminate tenured staff, nontenured staff were dismissed on the basis of evaluation in most sample districts.

## CASE STUDY FINDINGS: FOUR SUCCESSFUL EVALUATION SYSTEMS

From among the 32 survey districts, we selected four case study districts representing diverse teacher evaluation processes and organizational environments: Salt Lake City, Utah; Lake Washington, Washington; Greenwich, Connecticut; and Toledo, Ohio. We spent a week in each district interviewing the superintendent and other top administrators, officers of the local teachers' organization, school board members, parents, and community representatives. Visiting six schools of different types in each district, we interviewed principals, specialized personnel, and at least six teachers.

The four case study districts approach the task of teacher evaluation in different ways. Their approaches vary with respect to the primary evaluators and the teachers who are evaluated. They also differ with respect to the major purposes of evaluation, the instruments used, the processes by which evaluation judgments are made, and the linkage between teacher evaluation and other school district activities, such as staff development and instructional management. Finally, districts represent dramatically different contexts for teacher evaluation in terms of student population, financial circumstances, and political environment.

Despite these differences in form, the four districts follow certain common practices in implementing their teacher evaluation systems. These commonalities in implementation, in fact, set the systems apart from the less successful ones and suggest that implementation factors contributing to the success of these systems may also contribute to the success of others.

Specifically, these districts provide top-level leadership and institutional resources for the evaluation process, ensure that evaluators have the necessary expertise to perform their task, encourage teachers and administrators to collaborate to develop a common understanding of evaluation goals and processes, and use an evaluation process and support systems that are compatible with each other and with the district's overall goals and organizational context.

Attention to these four factors—organizational *commitment*, evaluator *competence*, teacher-administrator *collaboration*, and strategic *compatibility*—has elevated evaluation in these districts from what is often a superficial exercise to a meaningful process that produces useful results. With regard to commitment, all four case study districts recognize that the key obstacle to successful evaluation is time—or, more precisely, the lack of it—for observing, conferring with, and, especially, assisting teachers who most need intensive help. These districts create time for evaluation.

Evaluator competence, probably the most difficult element of the process, requires two qualities: the ability to make sound judgments about teaching quality and the ability to make appropriate, concrete recommendations for improvement of teaching performance. Supervision of the evaluation process provides the most important check on evaluator competence. All four districts have mechanisms for verifying the accuracy of evaluators' reports about teachers. These mechanisms force evaluators to justify their ratings in precise, concrete terms.

In the four case study districts, the teachers' organization has collaborated with the school administration in the design and implementation of the teacher process. The extent and nature of the collaboration between teachers and administrators in the four districts varies, but all have means for maintaining communication about evaluation so that implementation problems may be addressed as they occur.

In each case study district, teacher evaluation supports and is supported by other key operating functions in the schools. Evaluation is not just an ancillary activity; it is part of a larger strategy for school improvement.

## EVALUATING THE TEACHER EVALUATION SYSTEMS

The four case study teacher evaluation systems succeed in several ways. First, and relatively atypically, the school systems implement them as planned. Second, all actors in the system understand them. Third, the school systems actually use the results. In varying degrees, the evaluation processes produce reliable, valid measures of teaching performance and are used for teacher improvement and personnel decisions.

*Reliability* in evaluation refers to the consistency of measurements across evaluators and observations. The degree of reliability required of a teacher evaluation system depends on the use to be made of the results. Personnel decisions demand the highest reliability of evaluation results. Evaluation criteria must be standardized and evaluators must apply these criteria with consistency when the results are to be used for personnel decisions regarding tenure, dismissal, pay, and promotion. The evaluation system may tolerate a lower degree of reliability when the results are to be used for formative assessments or informational purposes.

At least three sources of variability may make teacher evaluation unreliable: (1) variability in how evaluators interpret what they observe or what criteria they stress in making judgments; (2)

variability in the evaluations of a single evaluator, i.e., whether the evaluator uses the same criteria and applies them consistently when observing different teachers; and (3) variability in observations, i.e., whether the evaluator uses the same criteria and applies them in the same manner when observing the same teacher on separate occasions.

Toledo's evaluation process addresses all of these potential sources of unreliability by using a small number of evaluators, a reporting process that fosters common assessment criteria and applications, and frequent observation and consultation. More important, the consulting teachers discuss their observations and evaluations with a review panel several times a year. Finally, the Toledo process increases reliability by limiting the number of teachers to be evaluated and by allowing the small group of expert teachers who evaluate them released time.

The Lake Washington, Greenwich, and Salt Lake City teacher evaluation processes require an administrator to evaluate every teacher every year. This requirement decreases evaluation reliability by increasing the chances of variability among evaluators and variability across evaluations and observations. Evaluator training helps to offset these sources of unreliability to varying degrees in the three districts.

The *validity* of a teacher evaluation process depends on its accuracy and comprehensiveness in assessing teaching quality as defined by the agreed-on criteria. Although school districts may seek to finesse the issue of validity by striving for measurement reliability in their evaluation process, they cannot ignore the validity of the process when they use its results as a basis for personnel decisions.

The criteria, the process for collecting data, and the competence of the evaluator contribute to the validity of an evaluation process. The purpose of evaluation—the inference to be drawn, the help to be given, the decision to be made—determines the validity of the evaluation process. In short, the process must suit the purpose if the results are to be judged valid.

The criteria for judging minimal competence must be standardized, generalizable, and uniformly applied. Finer distinctions among good, better, and outstanding teachers require nonstandardized, i.e., differential, criteria.

To evaluate *minimum competence*, the evaluator must be able to observe the presence or absence of generic teaching skills. However, to evaluate the appropriateness of teaching decisions, the evaluator must know the subject matter, the pedagogy, and the classroom characteristics of the teacher being evaluated. The evaluator's level of expertise must at least equal, if not exceed, that of the teacher being evaluated.

In Salt Lake City, Lake Washington, and Toledo, the presence or absence of minimal teaching competence, especially the inability to manage the classroom, triggers immediate help. Principals generally admit, however, that they spend little time evaluating teachers who appear to be competent, and teachers not subject to special help allege that their evaluations have not given them constructive criticism relevant to their area of teaching expertise.

To increase the validity of evaluators' judgments, all four evaluation processes require careful documentation of teaching behaviors resulting in unsatisfactory ratings. This documentation enables someone other than the evaluator to verify that the teaching criteria have been applied appropriately. In addition, they require multiple observations for evaluations. The Salt Lake, Toledo, and Lake Washington processes provide explicitly for multiple observations and devote resources in the form of evaluator time to that end.

Toledo and Lake Washington have taken aggressive steps to ensure validity. Toledo chooses as evaluators consulting teachers who are recognized by their peers and administrators as experts in their teaching areas. The consultants are matched by teaching area to the teachers they evaluate. Lake Washington trains evaluators in the same teaching principles that guide teacher staff development. This training enhances the correlation between the evaluators' judgments and the standard of practice adopted by the district.

Salt Lake City enhances validity indirectly by referring decisionmaking to a committee containing two experts. The validity of evaluation judgments rests on the consensus of the committee. The presence of a learning specialist and a teacher from the relevant subject area or grade level on the committee increases the prospect that defensible inferences about teacher competence are made.

The evaluation of *relative competence* must take into account the probable short- and long-run consequences of teaching behaviors and the substantive basis for teaching judgments. This type of evaluation depends on high-inference variables, which require the judgment of an expert observer.

Greenwich is distinguished by its emphasis on evaluating degrees of competence as it seeks to help teachers improve their performance. The validity of Greenwich's process rests on its ability to appropriately diagnose the individual teacher's needs and to accurately gauge progress toward more competent performance in the areas so identified. The Greenwich process continues to be relevant as the teacher acquires the ability to make professional judgments.

The *utility* of teacher evaluation depends in part on its reliability and validity, that is, on how consistently and accurately the process measures minimal competence and degrees of competence. The utility of evaluation depends also on its cost, that is, on whether it achieves usable outcomes without generating excessive costs. The results must be worth the time and effort used to obtain them if the process is to survive competing organizational demands. At least three types of costs—logistic, financial, and political—should be considered in assessing utility.

Utility represents a proper balance of costs and benefits. The benefits include the provision of data for decisionmaking, improved communication, and personnel improvement.

Toledo's evaluation process has high utility. It succeeds in helping teachers to achieve acceptable teaching competence, or in removing them from the classroom if they do not. It does both without disrupting the system's operations or lowering the morale of school personnel.

Three critical features ensure the utility of the Toledo process: (1) It is carefully managed, and it is conducted by evaluators who have no other, competing responsibilities; (2) it is focused and it uses limited resources to reach a carefully defined subset of teachers; and (3) it is a collaborative effort and it engages the key political actors in the design, implementation, and ongoing redesign of the process. Moreover, it shows a relatively low overall cost and provides substantial substantive and political benefits.

Salt Lake City's evaluation process, like Toledo's, has fairly high utility for accountability purposes. The utility of Lake Washington's teacher evaluation process for identifying, assisting, and, if necessary, removing incompetent teachers from the classroom is also fairly high.

The Greenwich system not only enables the school system to engage the individual teacher, it does so in a manner that relates directly to the teacher's daily professional endeavors. Thus, the utility of the Greenwich evaluation process results from its ability to tap teacher motivation and desire for self-improvement and to reward teachers' efforts by acknowledging their importance.

## CONCLUSIONS AND RECOMMENDATIONS

Our conclusions and recommendations constitute a set of necessary, but not sufficient, conditions for successful teacher evaluation. In practice, educational policies and procedures must be tailored to local circumstances. Consequently, these conclusions and recommendations may best be thought of as heuristics, or starting strategies to be modified on the basis of local experience.

Conclusion One:

*To succeed, a teacher evaluation system must suit the educational goals, management style, conception of teaching, and community values of the school district.*

Recommendations:

1. The school district should examine its educational goals, management style, conception of teaching, and community values and adopt a teacher system compatible with them. It should not adopt an evaluation system simply because that system works in another district.
2. States should not impose highly prescriptive teacher evaluation requirements.

Conclusion Two:

*Top-level commitment to and resources for evaluation outweigh checklists and procedures.*

Recommendations:

3. The school district should give sufficient time, unencumbered by competing administrative demands, for evaluation. This may mean assigning staff other than the school principal to some evaluation functions.
4. The school district should regularly assess the quality of evaluation, including individual and collective evaluator competence. The assessments should provide feedback to individual evaluators and input into the continuing evaluator training process.
5. The school district should train evaluators in observation and evaluation techniques, including reporting, diagnosis, and clinical supervision skills, when it adopts a new teacher evaluation process.

Conclusion Three:

*The school district should decide the main purpose of its teacher evaluation system and then match the process to the purpose.*

Recommendations:

6. The school district should examine its existing teacher evaluation system to see which, if any, purpose it serves well. If the district changes the purpose, it should change the process.
7. The school district should decide whether it can afford more than one teacher evaluation process or whether it must choose a single process to fit its main purpose.

Conclusion Four:

*To sustain resource commitments and political support, teacher evaluation must be seen to have utility. Utility depends on the efficient use of resources to achieve reliability, validity, and cost-effectiveness.*

Recommendations:

8. The school district must allocate resources commensurate with the number of teachers to be evaluated and the importance and visibility of evaluation outcomes.
9. The school district should target resources so as to achieve real benefits.

Conclusion Five:

*Teacher involvement and responsibility improve the quality of teacher evaluation.*

Recommendations:

10. The school district should involve expert teachers in the supervision and assistance of their peers, particularly beginning teachers and those in need of special assistance.
11. The school district should involve teacher organization in the design and oversight of teacher evaluation to ensure its legitimacy, fairness, and effectiveness.
12. The school district should hold teachers accountable to standards of practice that compel them to make appropriate instructional decisions on behalf of their students.

# ACKNOWLEDGMENTS

We thank the many educators and citizens who agreed to be interviewed for this study. In particular, we thank the personnel officers in the 32 school districts who provided us with an initial understanding of district practices. Most especially, we are grateful to the several hundred teachers, administrators, school board members, and others in the case study districts—Greenwich, Lake Washington, Salt Lake City, and Toledo—who generously gave us their time and insights.

Joseph Vaughan was the NIE Project Officer responsible for the Teacher Evaluation Study. His conception of the project and his advice were major influences. The members of the panel advising the study helped us immensely.

The report has profited also from the constructive criticism of our colleagues Richard Shavelson and Steven Schlossman of Rand and Gary Sykes of Stanford University. We owe a continuing debt to Shirley Lithgow and Nancy Rizor, whose typing and other assistance greatly facilitated the accomplishment of this project. Thanks are also due to Barbara Eubank and Rosalie Fonoroff. Erma Packman has made the reader's task a little easier.

Naturally, we remain responsible for this report; for any errors of fact or interpretation, we blame each other.

# CONTENTS

PREFACE .................................. iii

SUMMARY ................................. v

ACKNOWLEDGMENTS ....................... xv

Section
I. INTRODUCTION .......................... 1
    The Importance of Teacher Evaluation ........... 1
    The Focus of This Study ..................... 3
    The Methodology ........................... 4

II. A PRELIMINARY LOOK AT TEACHER EVALUATION . 6
    Conceptual Framework ....................... 6
    Survey of Practices in 32 School Districts .......... 15

III. SUMMARY OF STUDY FINDINGS ............... 26
    The Four Evaluation Systems in Review: Different
      but Similar ............................ 26
    Salt Lake City: Accountability in a Communal
      Context ............................... 27
    Lake Washington: An Engineering Approach to
      Instructional Improvement ................. 31
    Greenwich: The Performance Goal Approach in a
      Management Town ....................... 33
    Toledo: Intern and Intervention Programs in a
      Union Town ........................... 36
    Similarities of Implementation That Make These
      Systems Work .......................... 39

IV. EVALUATING THE TEACHER EVALUATION
      SYSTEMS ............................. 44
    Reliability ................................ 44
    Validity .................................. 49
    Utility ................................... 57

V. CONCLUSIONS AND RECOMMENDATIONS ........ 66

REFERENCES .............................. 81

# I. INTRODUCTION

**THE IMPORTANCE OF TEACHER EVALUATION**

A well-designed, properly functioning teacher evaluation process provides a major communication link between the school system and teachers. On the one hand, it imparts concepts of teaching to teachers and frames the conditions of their work. On the other hand, it helps the school system to structure, manage, and reward the work of teachers.

Teacher evaluation attracted new interest in April 1983, when the National Commission on Excellence in Education published *A Nation at Risk: The Imperative for Educational Reform*. Several of the commission's recommendations concerned with teaching would require teacher evaluation:

> Persons preparing to teach should be required to meet high educational standards, to demonstrate an aptitude for teaching, and to demonstrate competence in an academic discipline. . . . Salaries for the teaching profession should be increased and should be professionally competitive, market-sensitive, and performance-based. Salary, promotion, tenure, and retention decisions should be tied to an effective evaluation system that includes peer review so that superior teachers can be rewarded, average ones encouraged, and poor ones either improved or terminated (p. 30).

President Reagan's endorsement of merit pay thrust the commission's recommendations into the limelight and, with them, the need for a careful examination of teacher evaluation practices.

*Action for Excellence*, the June 1983 report of the Task Force on Education for Economic Growth, Education Commission of the States (ECS), echoed some of the Excellence Commission's recommendations:

> We recommend that boards of education and higher education in each state—in cooperation with teachers and school administrators—put in place, as soon as possible, systems for fairly and objectively *measuring the effectiveness of teachers and rewarding outstanding performance.*
>
> We strongly recommend that the states examine and tighten their procedures for selecting not only those who come into teaching, but also those who ultimately stay. . . . Ineffective teachers—those who

fall short repeatedly in fair and objective evaluations—should, in due course and with due process, be dismissed (p. 39).[1]

The ECS recommendations reveal a strong preoccupation with teacher competence. At the same time, they stress the importance of "a new and higher regard for teachers and for the profession of teaching" (p. 37).

Education policymakers increasingly consider better teachers and better teaching the key to better education. The Excellence Commission, seeking ways to improve the quality of education, recommended improving the quality of teachers. Exploring ways to restructure education to benefit economic growth, ECS also advocated better teachers. In September 1983, the Commission on Precollege Education in Mathematics, Science and Technology of the National Science Board, in its report, *Educating Americans for the 21st Century*, again stressed the quality of teachers and teaching.

As unremarkable as this consensus now seems, it reverses educational policy trends of the past two decades. The teacher-proof curriculum, test-based instructional management, and student competence testing initiatives were all based on the premise that education could be improved without improving the quality of teachers.

Teacher evaluation constitutes an important aspect of quality improvement. But, improving the quality of teachers and of teaching requires more than evaluation: It requires attracting highly able students to teaching, preparing them to teach, ascertaining that they can teach, providing an environment in which they can teach, motivating them to teach, and persuading them to remain in teaching. At the same time, quality improvement requires the introduction of quality-control mechanisms that do not distort the educational process in unintended and undesirable ways.

Proper teacher evaluation can determine whether new teachers can teach, help all teachers to improve, and indicate when a teacher can or will no longer teach effectively. We found, however, that teacher evaluation, properly done, is a difficult undertaking. As the results of teacher evaluation are put to broader uses, we may expect that the difficulties associated with teacher evaluation will increase.

The new concern for the quality of education and of teachers is being translated into merit-pay, career-ladder, and master-teacher policies that presuppose the existence of effective teacher evaluation systems. Many school districts will be reassessing their teacher evaluation practices; certainly, they will be paying more attention to them. School district personnel must understand the educational and

---

[1]Emphasis in the original.

organizational implications of the teacher evaluation system that they adopt, because that system can define the nature of teaching and education in their schools. In particular, the system can either reinforce the idea of teaching as a profession, or it can further deprofessionalize teaching, making it less able to attract and retain talented teachers.

In sum, before they introduce new policies for certification, tenure, promotion, merit pay, master teachers, and differentiated staffing, educators and policymakers will want the answers to such questions as:

- Can one teacher evaluation system reward superior teachers, encourage average ones, and improve or terminate the employment of poor ones? Can one system be used for teacher improvement as well as personnel decisions? Under what conditions?
- How does a person demonstrate an aptitude for teaching? Can this aptitude be recognized in a written test? Or must a prospective teacher be evaluated while teaching?
- What problems are posed by linking salary, promotion, tenure, and retention decisions to teacher evaluation?
- Can teacher evaluation be used by itself to select master teachers when master teacher is a rank like full professor? When master teacher is a role like supervising teacher?
- How can teacher evaluation be used by master teachers to supervise probationary teachers?

## THE FOCUS OF THIS STUDY

We designed this study to assess teacher evaluation practices with a view to analyzing how teacher evaluation can be used to improve personnel decisions and staff development. In this report, we describe four school districts that use teacher evaluation for these purposes. We discovered in the course of this study, however, that relatively few school districts have highly developed teacher evaluation systems, and even fewer put the results into action. This discovery suggests that most school systems will have to develop teacher evaluation systems before they can introduce innovative personnel practices.

The report explains how the *master teacher concept* operates in four school districts. It discusses this particular concept because the districts that we visited happened to use expert teachers (variously defined and titled) to help with teacher evaluation and staff development. Our report does not directly address the use of teacher evaluation results for merit pay and the selection of master teachers, because none of the districts considered for this study used teacher evaluation for merit pay and none used teacher evaluation results by themselves to select master teachers. Nevertheless, our findings provide important insights into the problems and prospects associated with these proposals.

## THE METHODOLOGY

The study began with a review of the literature (summarized in Section II) and a preliminary survey of 32 districts. We used a two-stage reputational sampling process to find school districts with highly developed teacher evaluation practices, obtaining nominations from the literature on teacher evaluation, members of our advisory panel, researchers, and practitioners. We conducted exploratory interviews in 32 sites, speaking at length with the individual having primary responsibility for teacher evaluation, and collected relevant record data, such as district evaluation goal statements, evaluation instruments, and collective bargaining agreements.

To select the case study districts, we considered demographic criteria, organizational criteria (e.g., degree of centralization), the district's primary purposes for teacher evaluation, teacher evaluation processes, methods and assumptions, and, after a preliminary assessment, the degree of implementation of the system. We finally selected four school districts representing diverse teacher evaluation processes and organizational environments: Salt Lake City, Utah; Lake Washington, Washington; Greenwich, Connecticut; and Toledo, Ohio.

Before visiting each school district, we reviewed the documentation pertaining to school district personnel and teacher evaluation policies. We then spent a week in each district interviewing the superintendent, the director of personnel, most senior administrators in the central office, and other central office staff concerned with teacher evaluation. We also interviewed officers and executives of the local teachers' organizations, school board members, parent and community representatives, and knowledgeable reporters from the local media.

In each school district, we visited six schools of varying grade levels, size, and neighborhood type. At each school, we interviewed the principal, other specialized (differentiated staff) personnel, and at least six teachers, including the teachers' organization building representative.

From central administrators, we sought an understanding of the political and organizational contexts, the origin of and motivation for the particular teacher evaluation process in use, the formal description of policy, and the uses to which results are put. From principals, we sought an understanding of how the process is implemented and how it affects their job and their ability to attain instructional and other school goals.

From teachers, we sought an understanding of how teacher evaluation affects the day-to-day life of the school and the quality of their instruction, and how they perceive the nature of teaching work in their district. From teachers' organization officials, we sought an understanding of how teacher evaluation affects management-labor relations and how they perceive the evaluation process with respect to thoroughness, fairness, reliability, and validity.

From community-based representatives, we sought an understanding of community perceptions of teacher quality and the teacher evaluation process. In all cases, we sought to ascertain general and role-specific perceptions of the teacher evaluation system and its function in improving the overall quality of instruction in the district.

Section II reviews teacher evaluation procedures in the light of various conceptions of teaching; it then provides an overview of teacher evaluation practices in 32 school districts. Section III summarizes the findings of the four case studies, analyzes the similarities and differences in the approach of the four districts to teacher evaluation, and describes what makes these approaches work.[2] Section IV assesses teacher evaluation processes as to their reliability, validity, and utility. Section V sets forth our conclusions and recommendations for the design and implementation of teacher evaluation processes that will work.

---

[2]These case studies are presented in greater detail in Arthur E. Wise, Linda Darling-Hammond, Milbrey W. McLaughlin, and Harriet T. Bernstein, *Case Studies for Teacher Evaluation: A Study of Effective Practices*, The Rand Corporation, N-2133-NIE, June 1984.

# II. A PRELIMINARY LOOK AT TEACHER EVALUATION

This section lays the groundwork for the case studies that provided the main data for the report. We review, first, the theory that informed the study and, second, the findings of a survey of teacher evaluation practices in 32 districts.

## CONCEPTUAL FRAMEWORK

We present here a conceptual framework for the study of teacher evaluation in the context of school organizations.[1] We examine the different conceptions of teaching and school organization that underlie teacher evaluation to determine whether teacher evaluation practices achieve the purposes for which they are intended.

Much existing literature on teacher evaluation examines instruments and techniques for evaluation without reference to their theoretical underpinnings or to the organizational contexts in which they are to be used. Without such reference, potential users—for example, school district administrators—cannot easily assess whether a particular approach will suit their purposes, conceptions of education, or organizational characteristics. Nor can they predict the effectiveness of the approach in achieving its purposes or its other likely outcomes. With theory, knowledge gained from other districts' experiences, and knowledge of their own districts, potential users can make informed estimates of probable local effectiveness and effects.

Teacher evaluation, if it is to work, must satisfy competing individual and organizational needs. It must balance the centralization and standardization needed for personnel decisions against the flexibility and responsiveness needed for helping teachers to improve. To make teacher evaluation work, districts must achieve this balance.

### Theoretical Conceptions of Teaching

A teacher evaluation system must define the teaching task and provide a mechanism for judging the teacher. Here we look at teaching as labor, craft, profession, and art. These four ways of viewing teaching by revealing the assumptions that lie behind different techniques for

---
[1] See also Darling-Hammond et al. (1983).

evaluating teachers provide a theoretical framework for analyzing teacher evaluation.

Under the conception of teaching as *labor*, teaching activities are "rationally planned, programmatically organized, and routinized in the form of standard operating procedures" by administrators (Mitchell and Kerchner, 1983, p. 35). The teacher is responsible for implementing the instructional program in the prescribed manner and for adhering to the specified routines and procedures.

The evaluation system of teaching as labor involves direct inspection of the teacher's work—monitoring lesson plans, classroom performance, and performance results; the school administrator is seen as the teacher's *supervisor*. This view of teaching assumes that effective practices can be concretely determined and specified and that adherence to these practices produces the desired results.

Under the conception of teaching as a *craft*, teaching requires a repertoire of specialized techniques. Knowledge of these techniques also includes knowledge of generalized rules for their application. Once the teaching assignment has been made, the teacher is expected to carry it out without detailed instructions or close supervision.

When teaching is considered a craft, evaluation is indirect and involves ascertaining that the teacher has the requisite skills. The school administrator is seen as a *manager* who holds teachers to general performance standards. This view of teaching assumes that general rules for applying specific techniques can be developed and that proper use of the rules combined with knowledge of the techniques will produce the desired outcomes.

Under the conception of teaching as a *profession*, teaching requires not only a repertoire of specialized techniques but also the exercise of judgment about when those techniques should be applied (Shavelson and Stern, 1981). To exercise sound professional judgment, the teacher must master a body of theoretical knowledge as well as a range of techniques. Broudy (1956) distinguishes between craft and profession in this way: "We ask the professional to diagnose difficulties, appraise solutions, and to choose among them. We ask him to take total responsibility for both strategy and tactics. . . . From the craftsman, by contrast, we expect a standard diagnosis, correct performance of procedures, and nothing else" (p. 182).

Standards for evaluating professionals are developed by peers, and evaluation focuses on the degree to which teachers solve professional problems competently; the school administrator is seen as an *administrator* who ensures that teachers have the resources necessary to carry out their work. This view of teaching assumes that standards of professional knowledge and practice can be developed and assessed and that their enforcement will ensure competent teaching.

Under the conception of teaching as an *art,* teaching techniques and their application may be novel, unconventional, or unpredictable. This does not say that techniques or standards of practice are ignored; it says, rather, that their form and use are personalized and not standardized.

As Gage (1978) explains, the teaching art involves "a process that calls for intuition, creativity, improvisation, and expressiveness—a process that leaves room for departures from what is implied by rules, formulas, and algorithms" (p. 15). He argues that teaching uses science but is not itself a science because the teaching environment is not predictable. In this view, the teacher must draw upon not only a body of professional knowledge and skill, but also a set of personal resources that are uniquely defined and expressed by the personality of the teacher and his or her individual and collective interactions with students.

Because teaching viewed as an art encompasses elements of personal insight (as well as theoretically grounded professional insight), the teacher as an artist exercises considerable autonomy in the performance of his or her work. Evaluation involves both self-assessment and critical assessment by others. Such evaluation entails "the study of holistic qualities rather than analytically derived quantities, the use of 'inside' rather than externally objective points of view" (Gage, 1978, p. 15). It relies on judgmental ("high-inference") rather than countable ("low-inference") variables, on assessment of patterns of events rather than counts of specific, discrete behaviors (Eisner, 1978; Gage, 1978).

In the view of teaching as an art, the school administrator is seen as a *leader* who encourages the teacher's efforts. The view assumes that teaching *patterns* (i.e., holistic qualities of a teacher's approach) can be recognized and assessed by using both internal and external referents of validity.

Obviously, these four conceptions of teaching represent ideals that do not exist in pure form in the real world. In fact, various components of a teacher's work embody different ideal types (e.g., motivating students, performing hall duty, presenting factual information, establishing and maintaining classroom relationships). Nonetheless, the conceptions of teaching signal different definitions of success in a teacher evaluation system.

The disparity implicit in views of teacher evaluation cannot be ignored. McNeil and Popham (1973), for example, make a strong case for evaluating teachers by their contribution to the performance of students, as measured by standardized test scores, rather than by the use of teacher process criteria. Millman (1981) also argues that "criteria and techniques for the fair use of student achievement in both the formative and summative roles of teacher evaluation can be devised." This view presupposes that students' learning as measured by their test performance is a direct function of teaching performance and it measures a teacher's worth in terms of the *product* or output of his work. Thus, it envisions teaching as labor and the student as raw material.

The vast majority (89 percent) of teachers, however, do not consider scores on standardized achievement tests a valid measure of teacher effectiveness (National Education Association, 1979). The views of most teachers are based on two notions: First, test scores are limited measures of student outcomes; second, other factors or dynamics of the teaching and learning process are at least as important in determining learning outcomes as the teacher's performance. These other factors encompass school and home conditions not under the teacher's control and the unpredictable elements inherent in human interaction that give rise to a conception of teaching as profession or art.

## Conceptions of Teaching in Teaching Research

Although the various conceptions of teaching differ along several dimensions, one can usefully view them as incorporating increasing ambiguity or complexity with regard to the performance of teaching tasks as one moves from labor at one extreme to art at the other. The role of the teaching environment in determining teacher behavior also increases in importance as one moves from labor to art. The more variable or unpredictable one considers the teaching environment, the more one is impelled to conceive of teaching as a profession or art.

Gage (1978) describes how the elements of predictability and environmental control differentiate teaching as a science from teaching as an art. Teaching as a science, he observes, "implies that good teaching will some day be attainable by closely following rigorous laws that yield high predictability and control" (p. 17). He goes on to say, however, that using science to achieve practical ends requires artistry—the use of judgment, intuition, and insight in handling the unpredicted, knowledge of when to apply which laws and generalizations and when not to, the ability to make clinical assessments of how multiple variables affect the solution of a problem.

Research on teaching parallels these conceptions of teaching in the degree to which predictability and environmental controls are assumed or even considered in the design and goals of the research. Some efforts to link specific teacher characteristics or teaching behaviors to student outcomes have sought context-free generalizations about what leads to or constitutes effective teaching.

This line of research strongly suggests that what teachers do in the classroom does affect students. However, assertions that discrete sets of behaviors consistently lead to increased student performance (e.g., Medley, 1979; Rosenshine and Furst, 1971; Stallings, 1977) have been countered by inconsistent and often contradictory findings that undermine faith in the outcomes of simple process-product research (e.g., Doyle, 1978; Dunkin and Biddle, 1974; Shavelson and Dempsey-Atwood, 1976).

Researchers have found that effective teaching behaviors vary for students of different socioeconomic, mental, and psychological characteristics (e.g., Brophy and Evertson, 1974, 1977; Cronbach and Snow, 1977; Peterson, 1976) and for different grade levels and subject areas (Gage, 1978; McDonald and Elias, 1976). Furthermore, interaction effects that may be identified in teaching research are not confined to easily translatable two- or even three-way interactions. This condition severely constrains their generalizability for establishing rules of practice (Knapp, 1982; Shavelson, 1973; and Cronbach, 1975).

Teaching behaviors that have sometimes proved effective when used in moderation can produce significant and negative results when overused (Peterson and Kauchak, 1982; Soar, 1972), or when applied in the wrong circumstances (see, e.g., Coker, Medley, and Soar, 1980; McDonald and Elias, 1976). This kind of finding discourages the development of rules for teaching behaviors that can be applied generally.

A more problematic finding is that the effectiveness of differing teaching behaviors depends on the goals of instruction. Instructional acts that seem to increase achievement on basic skills tests and factual examinations in many cases differ distinctly from those that seem to increase complex cognitive learning, problem-solving ability, and creativity (McKeachie and Kulik, 1975; Peterson, 1979; Soar, 1977; Soar and Soar, 1976).

We consider this finding related to goals problematic because if markedly different teaching behaviors lead to divergent results that can be deemed equally desirable, one cannot identify a single, unidimensional construct called *effective teaching*, much less delimit its component parts. One can, at best, pursue alternative models of effective teaching, making explicit the goals underlying each.

Clearly, the design of teacher evaluation systems depends critically on educational goals; as conceptions of goals vary from unidimensional to multidimensional, so conceptions of appropriate teaching activities vary from easily prescribed to more complex teaching acts resting on the application of teacher judgment. In short, as one ascribes different degrees of generalizability to effective teaching behaviors and different weights to context-specific variables, one implicitly embodies different conceptions of teaching. The more complex and variable one considers the educational environment, the more one relies on teacher judgment to guide the activities of classroom life and the less one relies on generalized rules for teacher behavior.

## Purposes of Teacher Evaluation

As indicated in Fig. 1, teacher evaluation may serve four basic purposes. The matrix artificially represents these purposes and levels of decisionmaking as distinct. In fact, teacher evaluation may apply to small or large groups of teachers (rather than simply individuals or whole schools) and may represent degrees of combined improvement and accountability concerns (as when promotion decisions are linked to improvement efforts).

Although many teacher evaluation systems are nominally intended to accomplish all four of these purposes, different processes and methods may better suit one or another of these objectives. In particular, improvement and accountability may require different standards of adequacy and evidence. Individual or organizational concerns also may demand different processes (for example, bottom-up or top-down approaches to change, or unstandardized or standardized remedies for problems).

| Level \ Purpose | Improvement | Accountability |
|---|---|---|
| Individual | Individual staff development | Individual personnel decisions (e.g., job status) |
| Organizational | School improvement | School status decisions (e.g., accreditation) |

Fig. 1—Basic purposes of teacher evaluation

Fenstermacher and Berliner (1983) illuminate these differences with respect to staff development (our improvement dimension), although their observations are applicable to accountability purposes as well. Their definition of staff development encompasses four scales along which approaches may differ:

> Staff development activities may be internally proposed or externally imposed, in order to effect compliance, remediate deficiencies, or enrich the knowledge and skills of individual teachers or groups of teachers, who may or may not have a choice to participate in these activities (p. 5).

According to Fenstermacher and Berliner, as participant roles and organizational levels become more differentiated, the profile of a staff development activity tends to shift from internal to external initiation, from an enrichment to a compliance focus, from participation by individuals or small groups to standardized programs for large groups, and from voluntary to involuntary participation.

For purposes of accountability, teacher evaluation processes must be capable of yielding fairly objective, standardized, and externally defensible information about teacher performance. For improvement objectives, evaluation processes must yield rich, descriptive information that illuminates sources of difficulty as well as viable courses for change. To inform organizational decisions, teacher evaluation methods must be hierarchically administered and controlled to ensure credibility and uniformity. To assist decisionmaking about individuals, evaluation methods must consider the context in which individual performance occurs to ensure appropriateness and sufficiency of data.

Although these purposes and the approaches most compatible with them are not necessarily mutually exclusive, an emphasis on one may tend to limit the pursuit of another. Similarly, while multiple methods may—and, many argue, should—be used for evaluating teachers, school systems must consider the purposes that each serves to ensure that teacher evaluation goals and processes do not conflict. In short, they must recognize potential conflicts before adopting a teacher evaluation system.

**Changing Teacher Behavior**

The primary goal of teacher evaluation is the improvement of individual and collective teaching performance in schools. To improve a teacher's performance, the school system must enlist the teacher's cooperation, motivate him (or her), and guide him through steps needed for improvement to occur. For the individual, improvement relies on the development of two important conditions: (1) the knowledge that a course of action is the correct one and (2) a sense of empowerment or efficacy, that is, a perception that pursuing a given course of action is both worthwhile and possible.

Most teacher evaluation processes identify effective teaching without addressing the question of how to change teaching behavior. The initiators of such processes assume that once they have discovered what ought to be done, teachers will naturally know what to do and will do it.

Fenstermacher (1978) argues, however, that "if our purpose and intent are to change the practices of those who teach, it is necessary to come to grips with the subjectively reasonable beliefs of teachers" (p. 174). This means creating internally verifiable knowledge rather than imposing rules of behavior. It assumes, first, that teachers are rational professionals who make judgments and carry out decisions in an uncertain, complex environment and, second, that teachers' behavior is guided by their thoughts, judgments, and decisions (Shavelson and Stern, 1981). Thus, behavior change requires transformation of belief structures and knowledge in a manner that allows for situation-specific applications.

A sense of efficacy is an important element of the link between knowledge and behavior. This sense affects performance by generating coping behavior, self-regulation of refractory behavior, perseverance, responses to failure, growth of intrinsic interest and motivation, achievement strivings, and career pursuits (Bandura, 1982; Bandura and Schunk, 1981; Bandura et al., 1980; and DiClemente, 1981). A sense of efficacy is not an entirely internal construct; it requires a responsive environment that allows for and rewards performance attainment (Bandura, 1982, p. 140). However, the individual must value the goals and the goals must challenge the individual, or the task performance will be devalued (Lewin, 1938; Lewin et al., 1944).

A review by Fuller et al. (1982) of the research on individual efficacy in the context of organizations suggests that, with respect to teacher evaluation, increased performance and organizational efficacy for teachers will result from:

- Convergence between teachers and administrators in accepting the goals and means for task performance (Ouchi, 1980)
- Higher levels of personalized interaction and resource exchange between teachers and administrators (Talbert, 1980)
- Lower prescriptiveness of work tasks (Anderson, 1973)
- Teachers' perceptions that evaluation is soundly based and that evaluation is linked to rewards or sanctions

- Teacher input into evaluation criteria, along with diversity of evaluation criteria (Pfeffer et al., 1976; Rosenholtz and Wilson, 1980).

These findings agree with those of Natriello and Dornbusch (1980–1981) on determinants of teachers' satisfaction with teacher evaluation systems. They found teacher satisfaction strongly related to (a) perceptions that all evaluators share the same criteria for evaluation; (b) more frequent samplings of teacher performance; (c) more frequent communication and feedback; (d) teachers' ability to affect the criteria for evaluation. Furthermore, frequency of negative feedback did not cause dissatisfaction, but infrequency of evaluation did.

Teacher satisfaction with evaluation, then, seems to rest on the perception that evaluation is soundly based, that is, that the teacher has some control over both task performance and its assessment. This perception influences the teacher's sense of performance efficacy (Fuller et al., 1982, p. 24).

Finally, opportunities for self-assessment and for reference to personal standards of performance strongly influence the sense of efficacy and motivation. The teacher evaluation literature has begun to recognize the importance of both self-assessment (Bodine, 1973; Bushman, 1974; Riley and Schaffer, 1979) and allowing teacher input into the determination of evaluation criteria and standards (Knapp, 1982). As Bandura (1982) observes:

> In social learning theory an important cognitively based source of motivation operates through the intervening processes of goal setting and self-evaluative reactions. This form of self-motivation, which involves internal comparison processes, requires personal standards against which to evaluate performance (p. 134).

## Teacher Evaluation in the Organizational Context

Recent policy analysis and program evaluation research to explain policy effects recognizes the importance of organizational considerations (Sabatier and Mazmanian, 1979; Sproull, 1979; Wildavsky, 1980). Formal policies and procedures, the research has found, may constrain, but do not construct, the final outcomes of any institutional endeavor.

The local implementation process and organizational characteristics—such as institutional climate, organizational structures and incentives, local political processes, expertise, and leadership style—determine the ultimate success of a policy in achieving its intended effects (Berman and McLaughlin, 1978; Mann, 1978; Weatherley and Lipsky, 1977). Effective change requires a process of mutual adaptation in which agents at all levels can shape policies to meet their needs—one in which the convergence of internal and external factors transforms both the participants and the policy.

The implementation of any school policy, including a teacher evaluation policy, represents a continuous interplay among diverse policy goals, established rules and procedures (concerning both the policy in question and other aspects of the school's operation), intergroup bargaining and value choices, and the local institutional context. The political climate of the school system, the relationship of the teachers' organization to district management, the nature of other educational policies and operating programs in the district, and the size and structure of the system and its bureaucracy all influence teacher evaluation procedures.

## SURVEY OF PRACTICES IN 32 SCHOOL DISTRICTS

As a first step in our empirical research, we conducted an exploratory assessment of 32 reputedly well-developed teacher evaluation systems. The following subsections describe the characteristics of the school districts, the similarities and differences in their teacher evaluation activities, some major problems in teacher evaluation, and some major effects of evaluation.

### District Characteristics

We surveyed local educational agencies (LEAs) in a broad range of rural and suburban districts, medium-size cities, and large urban areas. Minority enrollment in these LEAs ranged from 1 percent to 75 percent. The proportion of Chapter I eligible students varied from less than 1 percent to over 40 percent. District wealth as indicated by per pupil expenditure varied from $1400 to more than $3000.

Despite this substantial contextual variety, the sample LEAs had the following common features:

- All had a relatively mature teaching force—the average was 14 years of service.
- All but three faced declining student enrollments; all faced moderate to severe financial retrenchment. As a result, most had been required to dismiss teachers.
- Teachers were organized in all but two; 25 of the 30 organized LEAs had a collective bargaining agreement with their teachers, and 20 agreements included teacher evaluation. These agreements typically focused on procedural rather than substantive issues.

## Program Characteristics

The district teacher evaluation practices that we examined differed substantially in detail. These differences appeared primarily in local implementation choices—how to put a particular procedure into practice. District practices were remarkably similar in broad outline, however—indeed, much more so than we had expected, given the state of the art reported in the literature.

**Similarities.** Each of the 32 districts had had a teacher evaluation scheme in place prior to the present practice. In some districts, the former system was simply a paper activity—a routine task that occupied little time or attention. In the majority of districts, however, antecedent evaluation activities represented a serious concern on the part of LEA administrators and boards of education.

District officials and teachers had been dissatisfied with the way evaluation was conducted and the type of information produced. In particular, local officials criticized their earlier, typically narrative evaluation systems as too formal, too subjective, inconsistent, and inefficient. They sought to remedy these deficiencies with the present evaluation practices.

Interestingly, teachers strongly advocated a revised and a more standardized evaluation effort. In their view, narrative evaluation provided insufficient information about the standards and criteria against which teachers were evaluated and resulted in inconsistent ratings among schools—ratings that depended on the judgment of the building principal rather than uniform district objectives for teacher performance.

Although almost all districts initiated their present evaluation systems in an effort to develop a stronger and more consistent strategy, state-level action played an important role in the initial development of teacher evaluation in a number of LEAs. Many states have guidelines or legislation about teacher evaluation. However, these state-level requirements differ markedly in specificity and authority. In New Mexico, for example, legislation requires only that all districts keep records on personnel performance. Other states, in contrast, have specific mandates and guidelines as to the nature, frequency, and level of local teacher evaluation.

California, Connecticut, New Jersey, and Washington take a strong position on teacher evaluation, specifying the purpose and nature in some detail. Washington State goes so far as to outline the broad philosophy guiding its teacher evaluation requirements and to suggest a model to guide local practice. Connecticut, too, has taken a particularly active role by providing grants to support local development efforts.

Local respondents in these states cited state mandates as a major factor in the initiation and development of their teacher evaluation efforts. LEA officials with strong commitment to teacher evaluation were able to build comprehensive local activities on this state authority. In particular, thanks to state action, teacher evaluation is no longer discretionary.

The teacher evaluation practices that we examined shared—in addition to common reasons for initiation—a common process of development. With few exceptions, well-organized committees of teachers, administrators, union representatives, principals, and sometimes parents had instituted the new systems. These committees took, on average, between six months and a year to develop a teacher evaluation process and design instruments. Some LEAs relied on outside consultants—in particular, Richard Manatt, George Redfern, and Madeline Hunter—for advice and adopted their models in part or full. Most districts, however, developed their own evaluation practices without outside assistance.

Given the local origin of these teacher evaluation practices, they showed a surprising consistency in goals and criteria for evaluation. Our review of the literature identified four broad goals of teacher evaluation: personnel decisions, staff development, school improvement, and accountability (see Fig. 1, above).

These goals differ in theory: Personnel decisions involve teacher placement and tenure; staff development focuses on the identification of areas for teacher in-service training; school improvement concentrates on upgrading the quality of instruction; and accountability centers on setting and meeting LEA standards. Our conversations with district administrators suggested, however, that these differences are less apparent or meaningful in practice.

Asked to identify the *major* purpose of their teacher evaluation system, respondents in 12 districts specified staff development or school improvement purposes, 6 cited accountability, and 2 cited personnel decisionmaking. However, with only three exceptions, LEA administrators had difficulty specifying the primary goal of teacher evaluation. In practice, they asserted, teacher evaluation serves all four purposes. The differences among systems essentially reflected the somewhat different weighting applied by various LEAs.

The 32 districts also used similar criteria or categories of teacher competency. Although district practices differed somewhat in language or sequence, the majority of teacher evaluation efforts addressed five broad factors:

- Teaching procedures
- Classroom management
- Knowledge of subject matter
- Personal characteristics
- Professional responsibility.

Likewise, at a general level, the 32 LEAs employed similar evaluation processes. In 28 districts, the formal process called for a *preevaluation conference* between the teacher and evaluator in which evaluation goals were clarified and the evaluation process was specified. All districts used *classroom observation* to evaluate teacher performance and scheduled a *postevaluation* conference to discuss evaluator findings and reactions. In addition, 28 LEAs concluded this postevaluation conference with a *written agreement* between teacher and evaluator about a plan of action based on findings. In 26 districts, this plan of action included formal district *follow-up procedures*.

Districts also did not do many of the same things as part of teacher evaluation. Twenty eschewed *self-evaluation* as part of their procedures; 24 made no provision for *peer review*. Only one district had a system built on established *teacher competencies*. Only seven considered *student achievement scores* in the evaluation process, but noted that they did so more to indicate a problem than to assess teacher performance.

District teacher evaluation practices also showed similarities in terms of the locus of responsibility and source of funding. Responsibility for teacher evaluation, with few exceptions, was located in either the personnel division or staff development division.

Interestingly, the location of teacher evaluation responsibilities in one or the other division did not appear to signal substantive differences in LEA philosophy or approach to teacher evaluation. For example, some systems that emphasized teacher development and clinical supervision gave the personnel division responsibility for the program. In contrast, several districts that stressed teacher outcomes and categorized program goals in terms of accountability assigned responsibility to staff-development or support-service units.

With only two exceptions, financial support for teacher evaluation came from general administrative funds; it was not a line item in district budgets. Respondents saw teacher evaluation as part of an administrator's job and thus not requiring special funding. A number of respondents said that their teacher evaluation system "doesn't cost anything." However, as we discuss below, this approach may compromise teacher evaluation when these responsibilities are added to the other duties of central office personnel and building principals.

Finally, in 25 districts, the building principal evaluated the teachers in his or her school. In only a few districts did principals share this function with other district administrators, such as instructional supervisors. The number of evaluations required of a principal can be quite large, depending on the size of the school and the LEA's schedule for teacher evaluation. On average, however, respondents indicated that principals are responsible for comprehensively evaluating approximately 15 to 20 teachers each year. Preevaluation conferences, multiple classroom observations, and postevaluation briefings thus combine to make teacher evaluation a time-consuming chore for most building administrators.

In summary, at the broad levels of purpose, criteria, procedure, and structure, the teacher evaluation practices that we examined showed remarkable similarities. These similarities, however, masked substantive and significant differences in the ways teachers were actually evaluated. As we will show, these differences in implementation produced variations in the ways in which system participants perceived the evaluation effort and the extent to which it served its stated purpose.

**Differences.** LEA teacher evaluation practices differed in the type and amount of training given evaluators, the frequency of evaluation, instrumentation, level of integration with ongoing district activities, and the extent to which administrator evaluation complements teacher assessment.

Although only three respondents said that the district provided little or no training for evaluators, the significantly different level of training offered in our sample LEAs was bound to influence the confidence and competence of evaluators. Evaluator training ranged from low and infrequent to high and intensive. A district at the low end, for example, provided no formal training; instead, the LEA administrator responsible for teacher evaluation visited each school to talk with the principal about evaluation activities.

At the high end, some districts scheduled regular training sessions throughout the year, provided intensive in-service training in evaluation before school started, and brought teacher evaluation experts into the district (or provided funds for district personnel to travel to conferences or other districts). One district sponsored a Principals' Institute as part of its Instructional Improvement Program for Educational Leaders; teacher evaluation was a major institute topic.

The number of evaluations that a district required varied widely. For nontenured teachers, evaluations ranged from a low of once a year to a high of twice a month during the first year of teaching. For tenured teachers, some districts evaluated only when a teacher's contract came up for renewal (every three or four years); other districts evaluated once a year, with a minimum of two classroom observations.

The instruments used to evaluate teacher performance ranged from those using only a narrative form to those using a straightforward pass/fail measure of specified criteria. Most evaluation instruments, falling somewhere in between, used some form of scaling device. These instruments varied in number of points on the scale (3, 5, or 7), the extent to which they required additional evaluator comment or justification for a rating, and whether they included teacher response to evaluator comments. Together, these differences in the frequency and nature of teacher evaluation meant that district staff received significantly different types and amounts of information about teacher performance.

The local teacher evaluation practices that we examined also differed in the extent to which they were integrated into district activities or operated in relative isolation. For example, they differed in the degree to which adherence to district curriculum guides was an evaluation factor. For some districts in which it was not a factor, the disregard of curriculum guides in the evaluation process reflected the fact that, in the opinion of respondents, curriculum guides were underdeveloped.

Given that curriculum guides were fairly well developed, however, this diversity suggested variations in the district coordination of instructional management and evaluation. That is, LEAs that did not incorporate curriculum guides into teacher evaluation were unlikely to view teacher evaluation as a way to direct instructional practices. In contrast, districts that tied teacher evaluation to curriculum guides tended to see evaluation and instructional development as a piece: the goals specified in curriculum guides were expected to be addressed in the classroom.

Substantive relationships between staff development and teacher evaluation also differed substantially. Only five districts in our sample reported that teacher evaluation had no influence on staff development activities.

In only a few districts, however, were the results of annual teacher evaluations explicitly fed into the planning and design of district inservice education activities. In one of these districts, for example, the positions of personnel director and staff development coordinator had been combined into a single position to ensure close coordination between classroom practices and LEA in-service programs. Districts using a form of Madeline Hunter's clinical supervision model also maintained a relatively close relationship between evaluation criteria and staff development practices.

For most districts, the relationship between teacher evaluation and staff development was less clear and certainly less formal. Indeed, we inferred from respondents' comments that where a relationship existed between these two LEA activities, it was temporary and incidental.

Instead of the routinized and explicit coordination of teacher evaluation and staff development reported in a few districts, in most LEAs these activities appeared to function more or less independently of each other. Teacher evaluation seemed more nearly a "categorical" activity. On the face of it, this general lack of integration among teacher evaluation, staff development, and district curriculum guides raised questions about the effectiveness with which teacher evaluation activities could address such purposes as staff development and school improvement.

Finally, LEAs varied in the extent to which administrator evaluation operated in the same scope and depth as teacher evaluation. Respondents in 26 districts reported that annual administrator evaluations were required, often by state mandate. However, administrator evaluation practices were, for most of our sample, significantly less well developed than those involving teachers.

Typically, administrator evaluation consisted of a yearly narrative prepared by an administrator's superior. In only a few districts had administrator evaluation received serious attention and concern; these LEAs were reviewing teacher and administrator evaluation and were planning to develop a new system. In the remaining LEAs, however, the lack of attention to administrator evaluation suggested that this area was seen as separate and distinct from teacher evaluation practices.

In summary, the teacher evaluation practices that we examined differed substantially. Although these practices seemed similar in broad outline, they diverged as local implementation choices were made. Our preliminary assessment of local teacher evaluation activities led us to conclude that LEAs do not agree on what constitutes the best practice with regard to instrumentation, frequency of evaluation, the role of the teacher in the process, or how the information could or should inform other district activities. In our view, this lack of consensus signals more than differences in notions of practices appropriate to a particular setting.

These differences in practices, we believe, indicate that teacher evaluation presently is an underconceptualized and underdeveloped activity. Although almost all districts that we investigated had one or more particularly strong features, in only a few did teacher evaluation practices represent a well-developed *system* in which relationships among various evaluation activities were thought through and relationships between teacher evaluation and other district practices were established.

## Major Problems of Teacher Evaluation

Despite differences in level of development and diversity of local implementation choices, the major problems associated with teacher evaluation practices were similar in the 32 districts surveyed. Indeed, agreement among respondents about difficulties encountered in teacher evaluation underscores our conclusion that important conceptual work remains to be done in this area.

Two important problem areas may be inferred from respondent perceptions of teacher evaluation practices. Almost all respondents, even those who believed that principals supported the teacher evaluation program, felt that *principals lacked sufficient resolve and competence to evaluate accurately*. They frequently cited role conflict as the reason.

Central office respondents believed that the conflict between the principal as instructional leader and evaluator has not been settled. Noting that collegial relationships lead many principals to want to be "good guys," many respondents felt that principal evaluations were upwardly biased. Principals' disinclination to be tough makes the early identification of problem teachers difficult and masks important variations in teacher performance.

In addition, most respondents said that principals considered evaluation a necessary evil or a time-consuming chore. Since in most districts teacher evaluation has been added to a principal's responsibilities without taking other functions away or providing additional assistance, principals' perceptions of evaluation as a burden are probably correct.

*Teacher resistance or apathy* was the second most frequently cited problem. Teachers reportedly fully supported their evaluation program in less than half of our sample districts. Some teacher anxiety almost certainly stems from evaluation itself. However, by respondent report, a substantial amount of teacher discomfort results from a third problem area: *lack of uniformity and consistency within a school system*. Even though evaluation instruments have become more standardized, in many districts teachers believe that the present system still depends too much on the judgment or predisposition of the principal and leads to different ratings for similar teacher practices in different schools.

While inconsistency in evaluation judgments stems in part from instrumentation, it also reflects another problem area: *inadequate training for evaluators*. Many LEA respondents felt that staff responsible for evaluation did not receive enough training and that the training they received provided insufficient guidance in the conduct of evaluation.

Respondents also reported difficulty in two other areas: the evaluation of secondary school staff and the evaluation of specialists. Both issues involve *the difficulty of a generalist evaluator* (i.e., the principal) *assessing the competence of a specialist teacher* (i.e., secondary-level-chemistry, mathematics, language, and LEA art specialists, physical-education and vocational-education instructors, and the like). Some districts have sought to solve the problem at the secondary level by introducing a form of peer review. But most respondents felt that the inability of their system to recognize differences in elementary, secondary, and specialist teacher performance remained an important, unresolved issue.

## Major Effects of Teacher Evaluation

A number of respondents shared the view of the LEA administrator who said: "Teacher evaluation is one of the most powerful ways to impact instruction." The power of teacher evaluation as an improvement strategy is evident in the positive outcomes that respondents attributed to their evaluation system, even when they believed that the system needed revision.

Respondents consistently reported two results of teacher evaluation: *improved teacher-administrator communication* and *increased teacher awareness of instructional goals and classroom practices*. Even in the less-developed teacher evaluation systems, the process of evaluation—preobservation conferences, observation, and postevaluation meetings—substantially improved teacher-principal relationships and sharpened teachers' awareness of the goals and process of instruction.

Improved communication was mentioned frequently. One respondent said that teachers tell him: "This is the first time I have gotten meaningful help from my principal." Another cited teacher reports that the school climate had improved since evaluation responsibilities brought principals into the classrooms regularly. Still another said: "Teacher evaluation has brought about a sense of team effort at the building level that did not exist before. More teachers and principals are beginning to establish common goals."

An evaluation program reportedly gives teachers an increased sense of pride and professionalism and motivates them to improve classroom practices. Moreover, teachers take pride in their own support of evaluation and the professionalism that their support of evaluation implies. As one superintendent put it: "Our teacher evaluation program has made teachers prouder of their system. They are proud of their role in ensuring academic standards in our schools."

Respondents attributed part of this sense of pride and professionalism to the school systems' recognition of the teachers' competence. They ascribed another important part to the opportunities for feedback and discussions about standards of good practice that evaluation provides. In short, teacher evaluation has eroded the traditional isolation of the classroom teacher. It has improved communication, and it has given teachers a sense of task in the loosely coupled system of school districts, school buildings, and classrooms.

In most districts, the teacher evaluation system has also led to personnel actions. Although few LEAs used evaluation outcomes to terminate tenured staff, nontenured staff were dismissed on the basis of evaluation in most sample LEAs. Not surprisingly, LEAs located in states having particularly restrictive state-level legislation concerning termination of tenured teachers (e.g., New Jersey) have undertaken especially thorough evaluations of beginning teachers. However, more than half of our sample indicated that evaluation has played a major role in "counseling out" tenured teachers shown to be ill-suited for teaching.

Other reported results of teacher evaluation include: better LEA-teacher union relations; improved classroom instruction; student achievement gains; more funds allocated for staff development; and increased public confidence in the schools. The extent to which these outcomes can be attributed to teacher evaluation or, in fact, have occurred is discussed in our case analyses of four of these 32 districts.

## Issues for Case Study Analyses

The substantive difference in district teacher evaluation practices and the problems raised by respondents suggested a number of issues for our case study analyses. The role of the principal in teacher evaluation emerges as a primary concern. In most districts, the principal is the primary if not the sole evaluator of teacher performance. Yet respondents report that principals are overburdened, often inadequately trained, and constrained in their evaluation function by collegial relationships with their staff.

Practitioner concerns about the reliability and validity of teacher evaluations pose other central concerns. Many respondents pointed to insufficient differentiation among types of teachers as a development problem for teacher evaluation. Do available strategies allow for individual school or teacher differences?

Local respondents indicated that while their evaluation system had a primary goal, in reality it was expected to serve four goals: personnel decisions, staff development, school improvement, and accountability.

How realistic is that expectation? Can a single evaluation system address all four purposes equally well? Which approaches to evaluation best suit which goals?

Finally, according to most respondents, their teacher evaluation system "doesn't cost anything." However, even if teacher evaluation does not appear in an LEA budget, costs nonetheless are associated with it. These costs include not only dollars, but tasks done, however superficially, in connection with evaluation, management time devoted to developing, monitoring, and negotiating evaluation, teacher time away from classrooms or "off-task" in classrooms, and so on.

Local practitioners must balance LEA teacher evaluation purposes, district resources, and traditions. Our case studies analyze the factors central to resolving the dilemmas underlying teacher evaluation, in particular:

- Divisions of authority and responsibility among teachers, principals, and central office administrators in the design and implementation of the teacher evaluation process
- The degree of centralization and standardization of the management of the process
- Distinctions between the formal process and the process as implemented
- The extent to which the process balances control and autonomy, commonality, and flexibility.

# III. SUMMARY OF STUDY FINDINGS

## THE FOUR EVALUATION SYSTEMS IN REVIEW: DIFFERENT BUT SIMILAR

Salt Lake City, Lake Washington, Greenwich, and Toledo—the case study districts—approach the task of teacher evaluation in different ways. They emphasize different purposes for evaluation; they use different methods for assessing teachers; and they assign different roles to teachers, principals, and central office administrators in the evaluation process.

These evaluation systems nevertheless share implementation characteristics. These commonalities in implementation, in fact, set these four systems apart from less successful ones. Moreover, they suggest that implementation factors contributing to the success of these systems may also contribute to the success of other formal processes.

The four teacher evaluation systems vary with respect to the primary evaluators and the teachers who are evaluated. They also differ with respect to the major purposes of evaluation, the instruments used, the processes by which evaluation judgments are made, and the linkage between teacher evaluation and other school district activities, such as staff development and instructional management. Finally, districts represent dramatically different contexts for teacher evaluation in terms of student population, financial circumstances, and political environment.

Despite these differences in form, the four districts follow certain common practices in implementing their teacher evaluation systems. Specifically, they pay attention to four critical implementation factors:

1. They provide top-level leadership and institutional resources for the evaluation process.
2. They ensure that evaluators have the necessary expertise to perform their task.
3. They ensure administrator-teacher collaboration to develop a common understanding of evaluation goals and processes.
4. They use an evaluation process and support systems that are compatible with each other and with the district's overall goals and organizational context.

Attention to these four factors—organizational *commitment*, evaluator *competence, collaboration,* and strategic *compatibility*—has elevated evaluation from what is often a pro forma exercise to a meaningful process that produces useful results. Although these factors seem to be straightforward and self-evident requisites for effective evaluation, they are not easily accomplished and are usually overlooked in the pressure to develop and adopt the perfect checklist or set of criteria for teacher evaluation.

Moreover, the districts are striving to maintain and improve the organizational supports and processes on which meaningful evaluation depends. They understand that the implementation of the evaluation process is at least as important as its form. We summarize below the formal aspects of the four district teacher evaluation processes and how they operate in an organizational context.[1]

## SALT LAKE CITY: ACCOUNTABILITY IN A COMMUNAL CONTEXT

The hard-nosed yet relatively informal teacher evaluation process in Salt Lake City occurs in a state lacking a teacher tenure law and state-mandated teacher evaluation. The 25,000-student population of Salt Lake is relatively homogeneous for an urban district, and the dominant Mormon culture emphasizes education, conformity, and cooperative endeavor.

The concept of *shared governance* undergirding the teacher evaluation process conforms to Mormon community values. Management by decentralized consensus among parents, teachers, and administrators allows widespread input into nearly all aspects of school operations, including the assessment of teachers. Teachers are evaluated under a system based on communal decisionmaking with appeal to a higher authority.

Of the four case study teacher evaluation systems, that of Salt Lake centers most explicitly on making personnel decisions in the name of accountability. The *remediation* process to which principals may assign teachers judged inadequate has resulted in the removal of 37 teachers over the past nine years and the reinstatement of nearly that number of successfully remediated teachers to presumably more productive classroom teaching. Although principals initiate the remediation process, a four-member remediation team, composed of two administrators and two teachers, conducts the two- to five-month

---

[1] At the risk of oversimplification, we use metaphors to suggest the stylistic and substantive differences among the districts' approaches to teacher evaluation.

assistance and monitoring process. At the end of the remediation period, the principal recommends either termination or reinstatement.

The Salt Lake teacher evaluation system relies on an annual goal-setting exercise in which the principal and teacher confer on which system, school, or personal goals the teacher will pursue for the coming year. The system specifies neither the number of observations nor their duration. Observations may focus on either the adopted goals or a list of "teaching expectancies" included in the collective bargaining agreement between the school district and the Salt Lake Teachers Association (SLTA).

The evaluation system does not begin to operate in a highly formalized manner unless a teacher is performing poorly. Prior to formal remediation, a principal may initiate informal remediation, at which point observed deficiencies and a specified plan of action are put in writing, and the teacher is given additional supervision and assistance. If informal remediation succeeds, no record of the process enters the teacher's personnel file. If it fails, the teacher receives formal remediation.

## Organizational Commitment

The superintendent gives teacher evaluation and remediation high priority. He personally redesigned and manages these two elements of the governance structure.

A variety of mechanisms make a teacher's classroom performance a legitimate domain of interest for virtually all members of the school community. An "open disclosure" policy requires teachers to provide a written statement to parents of what they plan to do in each school year. Parents' involvement on school community councils allows them a voice in such matters as curriculum and staffing patterns.

In addition, a "review-of-services" process allows anyone to raise a complaint about virtually any school practice for investigation by a third party. About one-third of all teachers placed on remediation in Salt Lake were identified through the review-of-services process. Because of the openness of the system, poor performance is usually noticed and addressed by the remediation process.

The transfer and assignment process also draws attention to evaluation. When the superintendent negotiated an accountability system with the teachers' association, he traded job security for performance-based dismissal. Thanks to this agreement, the Salt Lake school system cannot lay off teachers because of declining enrollment or budget shortfalls; it can dismiss them only because of poor performance, if the remediation process fails. As a result, when positions are cut back in a school, some teachers—usually those who are performing poorly—are declared "unassigned" by the faculty School Improvement Council, and an assignment committee composed of teachers and administrators tries to find vacancies for them. Repeated lack of assignment due to poor performance receives scrutiny at both the school and central office levels and triggers the evaluation process.

The system provides additional resources for remediation. When a teacher is placed on informal remediation, the principal may call on one of 40 teacher specialists (who are chosen for their outstanding teaching ability) to provide classroom assistance to the teacher. When formal remediation is instituted, a four-member remediation team is assembled. This team includes the principal, one of five learning specialists from the central office, an SLTA representative trained to protect the teacher's legal rights, and a teacher with expertise in the particular subject area or grade level. The team may hire an additional expert teacher from a pool of those on leave or retired if still more assistance seems required.

## Evaluator Competence

Evaluation requires of those who implement it the ability to make both sound judgments about teaching quality and appropriate, concrete recommendations for improvement of teaching performance. Salt Lake achieves this dual evaluation function by dividing responsibility between principals and expert teachers. Principals are responsible for evaluating teachers and for instigating remediation procedures for those who are performing poorly. Once remediation begins, however, expert teachers in the appropriate teaching area assume a large portion of the assistance function. Salt Lake also operates a peer adviser program for first-year teachers in which skilled, experienced teachers receive small stipends and released time to help and to counsel new teachers.

## Collaboration

The Salt Lake Teachers Association collaborated with the board of education in designing the district's teacher evaluation system. In negotiations about the evaluation plan, the association gained a promise of job security for its members in return for accountability-based remediation and dismissal procedures. The SLTA developed the list of "teaching expectancies" that provide the basis for evaluation decisions.

The remediation teams include two SLTA appointees and two administrators; one SLTA representative is trained to safeguard the legal rights of the teacher on remediation. Although, originally, the entire remediation team had to agree to the dismissal of a teacher who failed remediation, more recently the SLTA has asked the principal to make the final decision after conferring with the team.

Other mechanisms in Salt Lake buttress the collaborative role of teachers in the teacher evaluation process and in educational decisionmaking generally. Teachers have an equal vote on instructional committees dealing with salaries, in-service training, administrator hiring, class size, and teacher assignment. Teachers have primary responsibility for curriculum development and for assisting both new and experienced teachers in classroom improvement efforts. The SLTA president is invited to attend the superintendent's staff meetings. Thus, teachers play a key role not only in the evaluation process itself, but also in all of the functions that support the implementation of evaluation.

**Strategic Compatibility**

Salt Lake City achieves strategic compatibility through shared decisionmaking rather than central enforcement. Like all other functions in the district, teacher evaluation relies on consensual decisionmaking, supported by the various mechanisms through which both teachers and parents can influence school operations. Decentralization in the context of shared governance permits a form of evaluation that is personalized rather than standardized, since the system opens performance to public scrutiny and comment, while its decisionmaking processes guard against unfairness.

In an effort to ensure that decentralized, democratic decisionmaking will result in the right outcomes for the system as a whole, the Salt Lake board of education recently sought to focus attention on systemwide goals by offering a salary increment to administrators for the annual attainment of these goals. It also made optional the earlier requirement that teachers set personal teaching goals. Many teachers had complained that the annual goal-setting process had lost its significance. Some called shared governance "shoved governance," implying that they did not have an equal share in decisionmaking. In sum, Salt Lake is still trying to balance democratic governance and centralized management.

# LAKE WASHINGTON: AN ENGINEERING APPROACH TO INSTRUCTIONAL IMPROVEMENT

Lake Washington, a well-to-do suburban district of 18,000 students, is growing in enrollment. At the hub of the Washington aerospace industry, the district's professional clientele understand an engineering approach to problem solving, and they support the superintendent's *integrated systems* model for educational reform.

Despite statewide fiscal retrenchment, per pupil expenditures in Lake Washington remain relatively high, in part because the district has received public support in passing bond levies for the schools. A large portion of the district's budget is used to support a variety of staff development activities centered on Madeline Hunter's *instructional theory into practice* (ITIP) approach. Skilled teachers designated as ITIP trainers help to maintain a uniform instructional approach in the district's staff development and teacher evaluation efforts.

In contrast to that of Salt Lake City, Lake Washington's teacher evaluation process is highly structured from beginning to end. Developed in 1976 in response to a state mandate, the evaluation system employs the state criteria in a checklist that the principal uses in observations of each teacher twice each year. Pre- and postobservation conferences accompany each classroom visit.

If a teacher receives less than a satisfactory rating on any criterion, the principal outlines a detailed personal development plan, which may include assistance from an experienced teacher, in-service classes, and specific reading assignments. If the teacher fails to improve, the principal places him or her on probation. During the probationary period, the principal meets weekly with the teacher to monitor progress toward specified performance levels. At the end of the semester, the principal, together with central office supervisors, decides the continued tenure of the teacher in the school district.

Although the professed goal of teacher evaluation in Lake Washington is instructional improvement rather than accountability, the system is designed to be used for making personnel decisions. District administrators claim that the evaluation system has resulted in the counseling out of about 40 teachers over a four-year period, a figure representing about 5 percent of the total teaching force in the district.

A concomitant emphasis on staff development and rationalized management are said to have brought a 20-percentile gain in pupil achievement scores over the same period. The cornerstone of Lake Washington's approach is the principal's role in managing the attainment of centrally determined goals and performance standards.

## Organizational Commitment

The superintendent began his term by stating that people are the most important asset that any school district has and that the most important people are those who work with children in schools. One of his first acts as superintendent was to eliminate 33 positions in the central office and to allocate the $700,000 in savings to staff development. That allocation rose to $1 million in 1983, about 2 percent of the district's total budget.

Staff development is tightly linked to teacher evaluation in Lake Washington. In addition to a 30-hour ITIP training course, teachers are expected to earn nine credits from in-service course work each year, and each school receives an annual allocation of $1500 for staff development.

Principals are evaluated on how well they manage staff development (including how many of their teachers have taken the ITIP course) and on how well they evaluate teachers. When a principal identifies a teacher who needs assistance in the classroom, he or she can call on one of five full-time ITIP trainers or the ITIP satellite teacher in the school, who receives released time to provide this assistance.

These resources are all brought to bear in the evaluation process. If a teacher is performing poorly, the mandated personal development plan will include specific staff development courses and ITIP trainer assistance in the classroom, as well as increased supervision by the principal.

The superintendent's emphasis on evaluation and his willingness to support principals' difficult decisions have made the process meaningful. Both central office administrators and school principals spend about 20 percent of their time on evaluation, and the same formal process that once resulted in no personnel decisions now leads to concrete action for improvement or termination.

## Evaluation Competence

As in Salt Lake City, principals evaluate teachers and initiate probation procedures for those who are performing poorly. Once probation begins, ITIP trainers provide most of the help to teachers needing improvement. These trainers are drawn from the ranks of Lake Washington teachers and are trained in instructional development.

Although evaluation and assistance function separately, the principals have also received extensive ITIP training. Thanks to this training, evaluators and trainers share a common understanding of good teaching, and the teacher in difficulty receives help that is consistent with the criteria on which he or she is evaluated.

## Collaboration

The Lake Washington teachers' association participated in the development of the district's response to the state teacher evaluation mandate. Although the district does not give teachers an equal voice in its operations, teachers participate in the evaluation process through the involvement of ITIP trainers for teacher assistance and of an association representative when a teacher is placed on probation. The superintendent meets with the head of the teachers' organization at least once every two weeks to discuss mutual concerns and problems, including but not limited to the functioning of the teacher evaluation process.

## Strategic Compatibility

Of the four case study districts, Lake Washington's engineering approach to school district management produces the most obvious compatibility, even consistency, among school improvement strategies. The school board's priorities translate into annual goals and performance standards for every staff position and for each school. Staff development, program evaluation, and teacher evaluation are closely linked by reference to these goals and by their common emphasis on ITIP principles and evaluation strategies. A highly rationalized process of need assessment, planning, and monitoring by which principals evaluate and are evaluated provides the tactical glue for these efforts.

The procedural and substantive uniformity that have contributed to the effectiveness of Lake Washington's teacher evaluation process now challenges its continued usefulness. As instruction has improved, the system has begun to recognize the need for differentiated evaluation responsive to individual teachers' skills and requirements. Adapting the system to provide incentives to already competent teachers will require striking a balance between the uniformity that permits identification of poor teaching and the flexibility that will inspire further development of good teaching.

# GREENWICH: THE PERFORMANCE GOAL APPROACH IN A MANAGEMENT TOWN

Greenwich, Connecticut, a wealthy suburban district of 7500 students, is populated largely by managers and professionals. The district's performance goal approach to school management and teacher evaluation reflects a managerial orientation based on incentives.

Operationally, the Greenwich approach means that, while centrally determined goals are used for school management decisions, the goals by which teachers are evaluated are not necessarily predetermined system goals. Each year, in consultation with the principal or teacher leader (a teacher with part-time administrative status), teachers set their own individual goals, plans for achieving the goals, and means for measuring whether the goals have been accomplished. Although teachers may choose system goals, the evaluation process is intended to foster individual improvement, and its design allows for individualized definitions of growth and development.

The Greenwich evaluation process includes at least one observation and three conferences between the evaluator and teacher each year. Teachers complete a self-evaluation report, and evaluators complete an open-ended evaluation report, which may be based on both the specific annual goals and on general teaching guidelines included in the collective bargaining agreement. Evaluation may result in a teacher's being placed on marginal status, but this rarely occurs in Greenwich—perhaps because of the evaluation process, or perhaps because the district's teaching force is highly experienced and highly educated.

The test of the Greenwich approach, given its individualized nature, is whether teachers say that it helps them improve their teaching. In recent surveys conducted by the district, about half of them said that it did. Because it operates carefully, the process forces regularized, teacher-specific interaction between principals and teachers and provides a focus and recognition for teachers' efforts. Based on a motivational theory of management, the approach tries to balance individual stages of development and system goals. Whether the process will adapt to the personnel decisions that may soon be required in this declining enrollment district remains to be seen.

**Organizational Commitment**

Teacher evaluation in Greenwich is emphasized in several ways. First, in recognition of the fact that evaluation takes time if it is to be done well, Greenwich has set a target ratio of 1 evaluator to 20 evaluatees and has deployed teacher leaders (who spend about half time teaching and half time on evaluation) to maintain this ratio in schools across the district. The released time and stipends of the teacher leaders translate into increased material resources for evaluation.

Second, both principals and teacher leaders are evaluated on how well they perform their evaluation functions. The assistant superintendents for elementary and secondary education read and critique each teacher evaluation report for its thoroughness and specificity. They also check to see how well the evaluations match up against the lists of marginal and outstanding teachers that the principals include in their annual school assessment report.

Improving evaluation performance will likely appear as a personal goal for a principal's annual review if it has received insufficient attention. Since teacher evaluation is the major administrative responsibility of teacher leaders, their continuation in that position is tied to their performance as evaluators.

## Evaluator Competence

In Greenwich, both principals and teacher leaders evaluate and offer recommendations for improvement. Their efforts are supported by 66 senior teachers, who receive released time and small stipends to assist and counsel other teachers on matters of curriculum and teaching technique. Differentiated staff—experts in different grades and subjects—provide specific help. Principals and other evaluators receive training and feedback on evaluation techniques in periodic workshops.

## Collaboration

The Greenwich Education Association (GEA) played a central role in developing not only the district's evaluation system but also the state's teacher evaluation requirements. The Greenwich system of mutually developed goals for teacher evaluation gives teachers a collaborative role in the evaluation process itself. This approach, instituted in Greenwich in 1971, was adopted in 1974 as part of Connecticut's teacher evaluation requirements at the urging of the GEA president.

The GEA helped develop the criteria for teacher evaluation found in the collective bargaining agreement. A district-level committee composed of six administrators and six GEA appointees oversees the implementation. This committee conducts periodic surveys of teachers' views of the process and makes recommendations for its continued improvement.

## Strategic Compatibility

Greenwich's interest in using teacher evaluation for multiple purposes is forcing it to confront the evaluation dilemma—the tension between the flexibility needed for teacher improvement and the standardization needed for system control and personnel decisions. Teacher evaluation and staff development have rested on a model of self-improvement based on teachers' personal goals. These goals are articulated in the evaluation process and pursued through both clinical supervision and individually selected staff development courses. In a sense, each teacher is evaluated against his or her own yardstick, appropriate to his or her stage of development and particular teaching challenges.

In recent years, the district's management-by-objectives strategy has begun to collide with the personal goal-setting strategy as centrally determined goals are accorded precedence. The district's plan to use teacher evaluation results as a factor in reduction-in-force decisions adds to tensions of individualized goal setting and assessment. These strategic inconsistencies may detract from the effectiveness of the teacher evaluation system.

## TOLEDO: INTERN AND INTERVENTION PROGRAMS IN A UNION TOWN

Toledo is a working-class, union town with a strong teachers' union. In the 1970s, a long-standing conflict between the school district management and the teachers' union, fiscal distress, and a lengthy teachers' strike led to a series of district school shutdowns. Only the concerted efforts of administrators and teachers to repair the rift by agreeing to share decisionmaking powers reversed the decline in student enrollment and public support for the schools.

As elsewhere, teacher evaluation in Toledo responds to public demands for evidence of quality control in the school system. The difference is that in Toledo the teachers' organization took the lead in defining and enforcing a standard of professional conduct and competence.

Toledo's teacher evaluation system differs from others in two important respects. First, skilled consulting teachers evaluate new teachers and experienced teachers having difficulty. Second, the evaluation process does not seek to evaluate each teacher each year. Evaluation resources are targeted on first-year teachers (*interns*) and teachers assigned to an *intervention* program. The consulting teachers observe and confer with these teachers at least once every two weeks for the period of the internship or intervention.

Principals evaluate other teachers annually until the teachers receive tenure, and once every four years thereafter. If a teacher qualifies for a continuing contract, formal evaluation ceases unless the teacher is placed in the intervention program. The principal and the union's building committee jointly decide the assignment of a teacher to intervention; the assistant superintendent of personnel and the president of the Toledo Federation of Teachers (TFT) must concur in the decision.

Although the express purpose of evaluation in Toledo is to promote individual professional growth, evaluation serves as the basis for making personnel decisions regarding contract status and continued tenure in the district. In the two years since the intern and intervention programs began, 4 of 66 interns were not rehired and 4 of 10 intervention teachers were removed from classroom teaching. The intensive supervision and assistance provided to intern and intervention teachers serves the individual improvement purpose for these teachers, but not to the exclusion of accountability goals.

**Organizational Commitment**

Top-level commitment to the evaluation process in Toledo is institutionalized in the form of an Intern Review Board, chaired in alternate years by the assistant superintendent of personnel and the TFT president. This board, which reports to the superintendent of schools, ensures the smooth functioning and continued improvement of the intern and intervention programs; it also serves as a forum in which deficiencies in the regular teacher evaluation process come to light at the top of the system. The composition and visibility of the Intern Review Board serve to direct attention to the evaluation function as it operates throughout the district.

Toledo has created time for evaluation by using consulting teachers as the primary evaluators of interns and intervention teachers. Depending on the number of teachers they are supervising at a given time, the consultants are released from classroom teaching responsibilities full- or part-time for up to three years. A full-time consultant may supervise no more than ten interns or intervention teachers at a time.

An annual allocation of $80,000 supports the costs of substitute teachers for consultants on released time, stipends and in-service training for the consultants, and curriculum and other materials used in assisting the interns and intervention teachers. These resources are devoted to the teachers needing the most assistance. Over the past two years, Toledo has spent an average of $2000 per intern or intervention teacher to provide this level of clinical supervision.

## Evaluator Competence

In Toledo, expert consulting teachers both evaluate and assist first-year teachers, but the principal files a summary evaluation report on the intern's nonteaching performance. The principal assumes the evaluation role after the teacher's first year. Consulting teachers are then used to provide classroom assistance to other teachers on a voluntary basis at the teacher's request (or principal's encouragement) or on an intensive and mandatory basis when a teacher is assigned to the intervention program.

The Intern Review Board selects consulting teachers after carefully screening candidates' qualifications, including teaching, leadership, and human relations skills. An in-service program prepares consulting teachers for their roles, and the Intern Review Board provides a mechanism for assessing the quality of consulting teachers' efforts.

## Collaboration

The Toledo Federation of Teachers was the primary initiator of the intern and intervention programs. The TFT president had tried to negotiate a peer review system for first-year teachers for nearly a decade before it was accepted as part of the 1981 collective bargaining agreement. The administration extended the concept to include an intervention program for teachers experiencing difficulty in the classroom. The principal and the TFT building committee together assign teachers to intervention.

The Intern Review Board, composed of five TFT appointees and four administrators, administers the intern and intervention programs. The board meets throughout the school year to guide the evaluation process and to oversee the efforts of the consulting teachers.

In a further collaborative effort, teachers in Toledo schools elect their department chairpersons and building representatives to staff development committees. At the district level, TFT-appointed representatives serve on all committees relating to curriculum, testing, and staff development. The superintendent and his staff meet at least monthly with TFT leaders to discuss educational policy development and implementation. Toledo teachers have a strong voice in virtually every area of instructional policy.

## Strategic Compatibility

In Toledo, thanks to a central balance of powers, committees composed of administrators, teacher representatives, and (in some cases) parents develop new strategies and policies for school improvement and oversee their implementation. Teachers' professional empowerment is expressed through union representation and bargaining power in top-level decisionmaking.

The prominent role of Toledo teachers in the intern and intervention programs contrasts with the traditional role of teachers in the evaluation process that has as its goal teacher protection rather than teacher participation. However, increased teacher power in the shaping of other teaching policies, including staff development, may ultimately increase their responsibilities as partners in educational improvement as well.

The Toledo school district, in operating on the basis of negotiated responsibility, is moving toward collaborative control over instructional quality. But because teacher responsibility limits management's decisionmaking prerogatives while also potentially undermining teacher protection, it can threaten both management's and union's traditional power bases. Thus, if this approach is to succeed, management and union will have to maintain a balance of their powers in all areas of educational policymaking. Otherwise, power struggles will fragment the educational process and defeat the public interest.

## SIMILARITIES OF IMPLEMENTATION THAT MAKE THESE SYSTEMS WORK

Each case study district has demonstrated organizational commitment to teacher evaluation, procedures for ensuring evaluator competence, collaboration with the teachers' organization and individual teachers, and compatibility of teacher evaluation with other district management strategies. These four factors underlie the success of these evaluation systems.

### Organizational Commitment

Personnel evaluation discomforts any organization. It contains the potential for misunderstanding, miscommunication, and anxiety on the part of both evaluators and those whom they evaluate. Good evaluation, however, offers the opportunity to improve organizational morale and effectiveness. It can foster concrete understanding of organizational goals and regularize communication among school personnel about the actual teaching work of the organization. It can also deliver the message that the organization needs these people and their efforts to accomplish its goals.

To make evaluation more than an isolated, peripheral activity, an organization must insist on the importance of evaluation from the top levels of the organization, institute concrete mechanisms for translating that insistence into action, and provide sufficient resources to the evaluation process. Evaluation cannot be considered an add-on function if it is to succeed. It must be a central mission for the organization, and it must be supported by resources that enable its results to be used.

Each case study district developed its own strategy for focusing organizational attention on the evaluation process. Although their approaches differ in specifics, they all recognize that a key obstacle to successful evaluation is time—or, more precisely, the lack of it—for observing, conferring with, and, especially, assisting teachers who most need intensive help. Time for these functions must compete with other pressing needs unless human resources for the functions are expanded and incentives for using those resources are continuous and explicit.

**Evaluator Competence**

Valid, reliable, and helpful evaluation requires evaluators who recognize good teaching (and its absence) and who know how to improve poor teaching when they find it. Evaluator competence is probably the most difficult element of the process. The best supported and most carefully constructed process will founder if those responsible for implementation lack the necessary background, knowledge, and expertise.

Evaluator competence requires two qualities: the ability to make sound judgments about teaching quality and the ability to make appropriate, concrete recommendations for improvement of teaching performance. If evaluation processes were designed solely to get rid of poor teachers, the second quality would not be needed. However, most evaluation processes also intend to improve instruction, and even those that strive for accountability must, in the interest of fairness, include a real opportunity for improvement before a teacher is dismissed. Thus, those who evaluate must both judge proficiently and help effectively.

The four case study districts all recognize this dual function of evaluation, and all, to varying degrees, divide the function between principals and expert teachers. In Lake Washington and Salt Lake City, principals evaluate teachers and initiate probation or remediation procedures for those who are performing poorly. Once probation or remediation begins, however, expert teachers—ITIP trainers in Lake Washington and teacher specialists in Salt Lake—provide most of the help to teachers needing improvement. Salt Lake also operates a peer adviser program for first-year teachers in which skilled, experienced teachers receive small stipends and released time to help and counsel new teachers.

In Toledo, expert consulting teachers both evaluate and assist first-year teachers, but the principal files a summary evaluation report on the intern's nonteaching performance. The principal assumes the evaluation role after the first year. Consulting teachers are then used to provide classroom assistance to other teachers on a voluntary basis at the teacher's request (or principal's encouragement) or on an intensive and mandatory basis when a teacher is assigned to the intervention program.

In Greenwich, both principals and teacher leaders evaluate and offer recommendations for improvement. Their efforts are supported by 66 senior teachers, who receive released time and small stipends to assist and counsel other teachers on matters of curriculum and teaching technique.

Several considerations underlie the division of evaluation and assistance between administrators and teachers who have been selected for their teaching and counseling abilities. The first consideration is time. Even a conscientious and competent principal who gives evaluation high priority has other administrative duties that compete for his or her time. He or she certainly lacks the time to help a teacher who requires intensive day-to-day supervision. Someone for whom it is a primary responsibility must provide the help for such improvement.

The second consideration in dividing these responsibilities—one often cited in the literature on teacher evaluation—involves the possibility that role conflict precludes one person's serving as both judge and helper. According to the theory, the judgmental relationships of evaluation inhibit the trust and rapport that a helper needs to motivate a teacher to improve his or her performance. This theory received limited empirical support in our studies.

To the extent that role conflict exists, however, it does not seem to operate in a simple, straightforward manner but depends, rather, on the evaluator's temperament, the incentive structure in the school district, and the prevailing ethos of the school. Nonetheless, some separation of evaluation from assistance (if only by the involvement of a committee rather than a single decisionmaker) seems to have proved a productive strategy in these districts.

The final consideration goes to the heart of the evaluator competence issue. Principals are not always chosen for either their evaluation ability or their outstanding teaching ability. In fact, an elementary school principal may never have taught in an elementary school, and a secondary school principal is not likely to have knowledge of all areas of the high school curriculum.

While principals may know or be trained to recognize the presence or absence of generic teaching competence, the task of providing concrete assistance to a teacher in trouble often requires more intimate knowledge of a particular teaching area than a principal is likely to possess. The logical solution to this dilemma is to assign the assistance function to one who has already demonstrated competence in an area of teaching expertise.

The use by the case study districts of a differentiated staffing model for teacher evaluation and assistance allows them to deploy district resources and expertise efficiently. In all cases, committees composed of both teachers and administrators choose the variously titled teacher experts on the basis of teaching competence and interpersonal skills. The expert teachers are assigned to provide as close a match as possible to the teaching area of the teacher whom they are to supervise and/or assist.

In addition, all case study districts provide some form of in-service training for evaluators on evaluation goals, procedures, and techniques. This training varies in emphasis and frequency. Lake Washington provides the most intensive evaluator training of the four districts. Principals attend a two-week workshop every summer which includes study of ITIP techniques, clinical supervision skills, and evaluation methods. During the school year, they attend monthly seminars that reinforce and expand on many of the same topics.

Ultimately, though, supervision of the evaluation process in each of the four districts provides the most important check on evaluator competence. All four districts have mechanisms for verifying the accuracy of evaluators' reports about teachers. These mechanisms force evaluators to justify their ratings in precise, concrete terms. Outside the formal evaluation process, mechanisms for controlling instructional quality—Salt Lake's review-of-services process and the school performance assessments in Lake Washington and Greenwich—increase the probability that poor teaching performance will be identified even when evaluation reports fail.

## Collaboration in Development and Implementation

In the four case study districts, the teachers' organization has collaborated with the administration in the design and implementation of the teacher evaluation process. The extent and nature of the collaboration between teachers and administrators in the four districts varies according to their political contexts and organizational characteristics. They have in common, however, means for maintaining communication about evaluation goals, processes, and outcomes so that implementation problems can be addressed as they occur. Consequently, evaluation is not an adversarial process, but one in which teachers and administrators work together to improve the quality of evaluation.

**Strategic Compatibility**

Most school districts function with a mixture of policies and procedures, some of which work together and some of which do not. These case studies support the idea that a process as fragile as teacher evaluation must be compatible with at least those other district policies that define the nature of teaching.

In each case study district, teacher evaluation supports and is supported by other key operating functions in the schools. Evaluation is not just an ancillary activity; it is part of a larger strategy for school improvement. The form and function of evaluation make it compatible with other tactics adopted to accomplish other district goals.

The success of teacher evaluation depends finally on the delimitation of its role in the school system. No single evaluation process can simultaneously serve all of the possible goals of evaluation well. Nor can evaluation serve alone as the tactical glue for diverse approaches to school improvement. In a practical sense, appropriate strategies for teacher evaluation explicitly address a high-priority goal of the school organization without colliding with other functions or goals. This means that the purposes of teacher evaluation in the organizational context must be carefully defined. It also means that new priorities may require explicit changes in teacher evaluation.

# IV. EVALUATING THE TEACHER EVALUATION SYSTEMS

The four case study teacher evaluation systems succeed in several ways. First, and relatively atypically, the school systems implement them as planned. Second, all actors in the system understand them. Third, the school systems actually use the results.

In varying degrees, the evaluation processes produce reliable, valid measures of teaching performance and are used for teacher improvement and personnel decisions. We examine below how the four systems attempt to ensure reliability, validity, and utility. In the course of this examination, we discuss the capabilities and limits of each approach.

## RELIABILITY

Reliability in evaluation refers to the consistency of measurements across evaluators and observations. To ensure reliability, some evaluation systems use a detailed observation instrument that specifies behaviors to be observed and guidelines for rating those behaviors. Other systems train evaluators to use the same criteria the same way for each evaluation. Still others develop a common standard and have evaluators discuss and critique each other's evaluations.

The degree of reliability required of a teacher evaluation system depends on the use to be made of the results. Personnel decisions demand the highest reliability of evaluation results. Evaluation criteria must be standardized and evaluators must apply these criteria with consistency when the results are to be used for personnel decisions regarding tenure, dismissal, pay, and promotion. The evaluation system may tolerate a lower degree of reliability when the results are to be used, for example, for formative assessments or informational purposes. Even for these purposes, however, reliability cannot be disregarded, for it affects both teacher morale and the perceived legitimacy of the process. Variability may replace reliability if the goal is to encourage individual development based on personally defined needs.

The case study districts use different methods and devote various levels of attention to reliability concerns. Of the four, Toledo's intern and intervention programs take the most comprehensive approach to ensuring reliability. Lake Washington, Greenwich, and Salt Lake City have a more difficult task because they use principals as primary evaluators and evaluate all teachers, thus increasing the number of raters, ratees, and observations to be standardized.

At least three sources of variability may make teacher evaluation unreliable: (1) variability in how evaluators interpret what they observe or what criteria they stress in making judgments; (2) variability in the evaluations of a single evaluator, i.e., whether the evaluator uses the same criteria and applies them consistently when observing different teachers; and (3) variability in observations, i.e., whether the evaluator uses the same criteria and applies them in the same manner when observing the same teacher on separate occasions.

**Toledo**

Toledo's evaluation process addresses all of these potential sources of unreliability by using a small number of evaluators, a reporting process that fosters common assessment criteria and applications, and frequent observation and consultation. The small number of consulting teachers who evaluate reduces the range of variability among evaluators.

More important, the consulting teachers discuss their observations and evaluations with the Intern Review Panel several times a year. Even consultants who have no current assignments attend the meetings. These discussions make the rating criteria explicit and concrete. In the discussions, the consulting teachers develop a common framework for rating teaching characteristics "outstanding," "satisfactory," or "unsatisfactory." The effect is to reduce variability across evaluations and across observations.

The use of a small group of evaluators in many schools increases system-wide reliability. Although evaluators may consider school context in judging the appropriateness of teaching methods used with a particular group of students, they are unlikely to accept a lower standard of teaching in one school than another. In a less centralized system using more evaluators, the evaluator's frame of reference may be only a single school and evaluations will vary more.

Finally, frequent classroom observation enhances the reliability of the process. (They also heighten its validity.) Evaluation based on observations made at least twice a month over the course of an entire school year eliminates the common complaint that a single observation cannot adequately measure teaching ability. The equally intensive consultation process, which incorporates joint goal setting and problem solving, also increases the probability that evaluator and evaluatee will arrive at a common understanding of what is being observed and evaluated.

The Toledo intern and intervention programs also increase reliability by limiting the number of teachers to be evaluated and by allowing the small group of expert teachers who evaluate them released time. Thus, the evaluator is able to work intensively with the teacher being evaluated.

**Lake Washington**

The Lake Washington, Greenwich, and Salt Lake City teacher evaluation processes require an administrator to evaluate every teacher every year. This requirement decreases evaluation reliability by increasing the chances of variability among evaluators and variability across evaluations and observations. Evaluator training helps to offset these sources of unreliability to varying degrees in the three districts.

In Lake Washington, principals receive ongoing training in ITIP principles, clinical supervision, and observation techniques. This training enables evaluators to interpret what they observe in similar ways. Most teachers and administrators in Lake Washington feel that, with a few exceptions, principals make fair and consistent assessments and that the standards do not vary widely from school to school.

The "evaluative criteria checklist" in Lake Washington is also intended to promote reliability by specifying 29 behaviors to be observed under the seven evaluation criteria. Since the evaluators must rate each behavior listed on the checklist, the instrument helps to focus their attention on these aspects of teaching. Although the behaviors are not precisely defined (they include, for example, "develops plans," "teaches the curriculum," and "prepares materials"), the list may prevent evaluators from ignoring certain teaching activities or from applying the criteria unevenly to different teachers.

However, the requirement that all teachers be evaluated each year decreases the time that an evaluator can devote to any one teacher. As a result, teachers who are having obvious difficulty receive more attention than those who are not. As one principal put it:

> I have to evaluate too many people. Four or five people are taking all of my attention and I am just doing lip service for the rest. There is no way to fit all of this in within the present system and state constraints. So I just go through the motions with half of them.

Perfunctory evaluation reduces the reliability of judgments. Principals acknowledge that some teachers escape being placed on probation because evaluators cannot afford the time it takes to administer the probationary process. Overextension of the evaluator's time results in unreliability across evaluations.

## Greenwich

Greenwich became concerned about reliability in evaluation when it faced the prospect of using evaluation results for making personnel decisions related to reductions-in-force. The evaluation process was originally intended to allow for varying standards of progress depending on teachers' felt needs and stages of development. That conception required reliability across observations of a single teacher but not especially across evaluations of different teachers or even among evaluators as a group.

The flexible character of the Greenwich evaluation process shows in the instrument used and the way in which criteria are applied. The evaluation form includes three spaces, labeled "description of observation," "summary comments," and "teacher comments." It lacks a checklist and specific ratings to be applied.

Evaluators may, however, draw on a list of guidelines for professional performance as deemed appropriate. The guidelines include aspects of performance ranging from "shows evidence of planning and good organization" to "interprets educational programs, procedures, and plans to the public," "has mature understanding of own and others' problems," and "conducts self in an ethical manner." These are high-inference variables, some of which are not easily observable. The guidelines are used selectively in conjunction with mutually developed individual teacher goals as criteria for evaluation.

This process provides evaluation of low reliability because the criteria and the manner in which they are applied vary (intentionally) from teacher to teacher. Low reliability does not invalidate the process for its intended purpose of individual staff improvement, but it limits the applicability of the process to other purposes that would require more highly standardized comparisons of teachers.

The most important feature of the process for individual staff improvement is reliability across observations of a single teacher. If the evaluator is to gauge progress, he or she must apply the selected, individually pertinent criteria consistently across observations.

Several features of the Greenwich process encourage this type of reliability: the teacher's development of an achievement plan and assessment criteria, the requirement that the goals be measurable or observable, and the year-end assessment by both the evaluator and teacher as to whether the goals have been "fully" or "partly accomplished" or "missed." However, the evaluator's summary observation is expected to include observations about other aspects of the teacher's performance.

As teacher evaluation has acquired new purposes in Greenwich, administrators have made efforts to enhance the other forms of reliability. Central office supervisors read and critique all evaluations for their clarity and precision of description. Training sessions for evaluators focus on critical discussion of these evaluations to improve observation and reporting practices so that the reports provide more concrete and potentially generalizable information.

At the end of each school year, principals must include lists of "outstanding" and "marginal" teachers in their school assessment documents. Efforts are made in the training sessions to assess whether the evaluation reports for teachers identified as marginal or outstanding contain adequate data for these judgments.[1]

## Salt Lake City

Salt Lake City's regular, preremediation evaluation process resembles that used in Greenwich, including its sources of unreliability. The Salt Lake evaluation process lacks observation instruments and checklists to guide the annual principal-teacher conference and classroom observation. At the conference, the principal and teacher consider which of a list of system-wide, school-wide, or personal goals the teacher will focus on for the year.

The decentralized management structure in Salt Lake, which produces different school goals and emphases, also encourages diverse standards for teacher evaluation. As in Greenwich, the evaluation process does not apply standardized criteria uniformly across teachers. Unlike in Greenwich, principals do not receive ongoing evaluation training to enhance reliability across evaluators.

The decisionmaking process for placing a teacher on remediation is not standardized. However, once a teacher is placed on remediation, some standardizing elements are introduced into the process. The central office selects one representative for each remediation team from a small pool of five *learning specialists*. The learning specialists bring a measure of consistency to the process because each serves on multiple remediation teams (thereby increasing reliability across evaluations) and, presumably, they share a common viewpoint about the goals and conduct of the remediation process.

However, the two SLTA-appointed representatives on the remediation team are drawn from a large pool. They bring less consistency to the process because each member serves on fewer teams and they receive no training to offset different views of evaluation and good teaching. The principal is the fourth member of the team and the final decisionmaker as to the success or failure of remediation. The team's

---

[1]Although the evaluation process may be used to place a teacher on marginal status, which would trigger a more intensive series of observations and counseling, this feature of the evaluation process is rarely used.

involvement is intended to increase the reliability of that decisionmaking process by countering the biases held by any single member.

The multiple views of the team members may also help rationalize the application of evaluation criteria to teachers on remediation. A list of "Teaching Expectancies" is used to guide the remediation effort, but it is difficult to use for diagnosis because it combines behaviors (e.g., "adjusts techniques to different learning styles"), outcomes (e.g., "evidence that student is working at task"), attitudes (e.g., "all students can learn"), and school conditions (e.g., "availability of resources personnel") in a single list. Such criteria are difficult to apply reliably.

The team approach for personnel decisions is necessary in Salt Lake to offset the other sources of unreliability in the evaluation process. It reduces arbitrary decisionmaking and obtains agreement about the appropriateness of an important personnel action. Thus, it has political as well as methodological value.

In sum, an effective evaluation system needs more than reliability. In fact, depending on the major goals of evaluation, it may not require reliability. A highly standardized, reliable process may not even suit some purposes. In the next section, we discuss validity and how the purposes of evaluation must guide judgments of its validity.

## VALIDITY

The validity of a teacher evaluation process depends on its accuracy and comprehensiveness in assessing teaching quality as defined by the agreed-on criteria. Although LEAs may seek to finesse the issue of validity by striving for measurement reliability in their evaluation process, they cannot ignore the validity of the process when they use its results as a basis for personnel decisions.

The criteria, the process for collecting data, and the competence of the evaluator contribute to the validity of an evaluation process. The purpose of evaluation—the inference to be drawn, the help to be given, the decision to be made—determines the validity of the evaluation process. In short, the process must suit the purpose if the results are to be judged valid.

The criteria for judging minimal competence must be standardized, generalizable, and uniformly applied. Finer distinctions among good, better, and outstanding teachers require nonstandardized, i.e., differential, criteria.

Teaching research has demonstrated that effective teaching behaviors vary for different grade levels, subject areas, types of students, and instructional goals. Thus, relative teacher competence cannot be assessed on the basis of highly specified, uniform criteria. When a school district adopts a single set of broad criteria, it must differentiate these criteria for specific applications. Excellence above all must be measured by broad, nonstandardized criteria.

Teaching competence may be conceived as a continuum. The further one moves along the continuum from minimal competence to excellence, the more wide-ranging and inferential the sources of data and the less uniform and generalizable the specific indicators.

The absolute minimum requirement for acceptable teaching is the ability to run a nondisruptive classroom. Our studies revealed that, more than any other problem, a disruptive classroom will trigger a special evaluation of a teacher. A teacher who cannot manage a classroom is presumed not to be teaching and to be creating a disturbance that disrupts the school. A disturbance that becomes visible outside the school disrupts organizational stability. Thus, teachers who lose control of the classroom are the first to be identified for possible separation.

Beyond acceptable classroom management, minimal competence demands mastery of subject matter and a repertoire of teaching techniques. Ideally, a teacher will not be fully certified until he or she has mastered both. Many teacher evaluation processes focus on assessing minimal competence.

Beyond minimal competence, a teacher must not only master subject matter and the repertoire of techniques but also must make appropriate judgments about when those techniques should be applied. This quality makes teaching a profession. A professional teacher has sufficient knowledge of subject matter and techniques to make appropriate decisions about instructional content and delivery for different students and classes. In other words, the professional teacher is able to ascertain students' needs and to meet them.

Beyond the ability to make appropriate teaching decisions lies the ability to diagnose unusually difficult learning problems, to deliver an unusually wide variety of instruction, and to inspire unusually creative or analytical thinking by students. This quality is excellence in teaching, which, like excellence in all fields of human endeavor, is rare.

The demands of evaluation differ along this continuum. The evaluator needs no special expertise to recognize that a classroom is out of control. To evaluate minimum competence, the evaluator must be able to observe the presence or absence of generic teaching skills. However, to evaluate the appropriateness of teaching decisions, the evaluator must know the subject matter, the pedagogy, and the classroom characteristics of the teacher being evaluated. The evaluator's level of expertise must at least equal, if not exceed, that of the teacher being evaluated.

As in other professions, judgments of the appropriateness of teaching decisions must rely on prevailing standards of practice. The judgment of excellence in teaching, however, must be based on superior standards of practice. Thus, the evaluator must have a high level of expertise to judge excellence.

All four case study districts claim to hold a professional conception of teaching. Yet their evaluation processes conform to this conception in varying aspects and to varying degrees. What the processes seek to measure and what they actually measure depends on who is being evaluated, by whom, and for what purpose. Those who are receiving intensive supervision are evaluated differently, at least in degree, from those whose performance is merely being checked. Those subject to an imminent personnel decision are evaluated differently from those who are not; evaluations made by generalist administrators differ from evaluations made by teaching specialists.

Although differential evaluation emphasis is valid, serious problems arise when a process that is valid for one purpose is applied to other purposes or goals. A process that produces a valid measure of incompetence may ill suit the measurement of degrees of competence. A process that reveals the extent of improvement in particular competences or areas of performance may not work for ranking teachers according to overall competence. Thus, in adopting a teacher evaluation system, a school district must ensure that the system suits its evaluation goals.

In discussing the validity of the teacher evaluation processes in our four case study districts, we distinguish between how the processes function for determining both minimal competence and degrees of competence. An LEA should base tenure and dismissal decisions on minimal competence. It should determine the degree of competence as a basis for helping teachers improve and making performance-related promotion and pay decisions.

## Evaluation of Minimal Competence

For the most part, evaluation by administrators in the case study districts stops short of judging professional competence as we have defined it above. In Salt Lake City, Lake Washington, and Toledo, the presence or absence of minimal teaching competence, especially the inability to manage the classroom, triggers remediation, probation, or intervention. Most of the teachers placed in these programs cannot control a classroom. The lack of pedagogical knowledge or sophistication may not, by itself, result in special treatment by the evaluation process.

Indeed, in all of these systems, principals admit that they spend little time evaluating teachers who appear to be competent; teachers not subject to special treatment allege that their evaluations have not given them constructive criticism relevant to their area of teaching expertise. Competent teachers do not necessarily consider the process useless. Rather, they criticize evaluations for providing too few observations and evaluators for making comments that fail to relate specifically to the pedagogical demands of their particular teaching assignment.

These criticisms do not indict the validity of evaluation systems; they indicate, however, that the systems are not especially designed to produce valid measures of the *degree* to which teachers have attained teaching competence in their particular areas of expertise. The strength of the processes lies in their ability to identify teacher incompetence. With respect to this purpose, the processes enhance the validity of evaluators' judgments in two ways.

First, all four evaluation processes require careful documentation of teaching behaviors resulting in unsatisfactory ratings. This documentation enables someone other than the evaluator to verify that the teaching criteria have been applied appropriately. The use of multiple observers by Salt Lake's remediation teams helps to foster objectivity. In Lake Washington, evaluator training in ITIP principles (focusing on a process of teaching that purportedly transcends subject matter differences) provides a common framework for evaluation judgments. In Toledo, a committee decides on intervention and judges how the intervention process is progressing.

Second, the districts require multiple observations for evaluations. If inferences about teaching competence are to support personnel decisions, they must be based on an adequate sample of teaching performance. Because the goal of evaluation is to certify minimal competence and whether the teacher under observation is progressing toward achieving minimal competence, evaluators must be able to assess the generalizability of observed behaviors. The processes for remediation, intervention, and probation in Salt Lake, Toledo, and Lake Washington provide explicitly for multiple observations and devote resources in the form of evaluator time toward that end.

The criteria and instruments used in these three districts bear only indirectly on the judgment of minimal competence. The criteria include instructional skill (generically defined to mean the ability to plan, organize, deliver, and evaluate instruction, to help students develop good work habits, etc.); classroom control and discipline; subject matter knowledge (e.g., keeping abreast of new ideas); and personal characteristics (e.g., dependability). The checklists include behaviors (e.g., "teaches the curriculum"), competences (e.g., "ability to motivate"), and outcomes (e.g., "student behavior demonstrates acceptance of learning experience").

One can question whether specific items on the checklists are necessary or sufficient conditions for judging teacher competence. For example, does the presence of lesson plans mean teacher competence? Does the failure to follow the curriculum guide mean teacher incompetence? Does the degree of student disruptiveness or passivity reflect the competence of the teacher?

In reality, evaluators judge incompetence as a whole, and the specified criteria have less bearing on the validity of the judgment than does the competence of the evaluator. Applying the criteria in a way that results in a defensible inference requires expertise on the part of the evaluator. The checklists merely focus the evaluator's attention on specific behaviors to be observed. The evaluator most likely makes a judgment and then rationalizes it against the checklist criteria.

Toledo and Lake Washington have taken aggressive steps to ensure validity. Toledo chooses consulting teachers because they are recognized by their peers and administrators as experts in their teaching areas. The consultants are matched by teaching area to the interns they evaluate. Furthermore, the Intern Review Board forces the consulting teachers to make clear the standards of practice implicit in their judgments by requiring documentation of teaching events, suggestions made, and concrete reasons for outstanding or unsatisfactory ratings. Consulting teachers must demonstrate their ability to relate observed behaviors to competence ratings.

Lake Washington trains evaluators in the same teaching principles that guide teacher staff development. This training enhances the correlation between the evaluators' judgments and the standard of practice adopted by the district. To the extent that the ITIP principles themselves are valid indexes of teacher competence, this training enhances the validity of the teacher evaluation process. It creates a common language among principals, teachers, and trainers. The common training and resultant shared language allow evaluators to communicate their observations and assessments with concrete, readily understood referents.

Salt Lake City enhances validity indirectly by referring decisionmaking to a committee containing two experts. The validity of evaluation judgments rests on the consensus of the committee. The presence of a learning specialist and a teacher from the relevant subject area or grade level on the committee increases the prospect that defensible inferences about teacher competence are made.

The evaluation of minimal competence, based on periodic observations of classroom performance, attends to the effective control of students and to the presence of certain teaching behaviors. These behaviors relate to planning, setting objectives, teaching a lesson related to the objectives, and evaluating whether the objectives have been attained. These low-inference variables suffice for judging minimal competence, and a moderately skilled observer can judge them.

This type of evaluation does not address pedagogical knowledge and judgment. Pedagogical knowledge and judgment relate to the appropriateness of teaching objectives for meeting certain goals or for different types of students, the relative effectiveness of alternative strategies for presenting particular types of content, the relationship among lessons taught throughout the course of a week, a month, or a semester, the variability of teaching techniques, the theoretical soundness of content and strategy decisions, and the depth of subject matter knowledge possessed by the teacher and imparted to the student.

The evaluation of minimal competence also treats neither creativity and innovation in teaching nor student motivation beyond the ability to induce compliance with work requirements. Furthermore, it ignores the multiple, long-term consequences for students of the overall classroom experience, such as continued enthusiasm for learning, broadening of learning styles, the ability to apply concepts or developed skills to diverse situations later on, and increased self-confidence. In short, evaluation for judging minimal competence attends to the form rather than the substance and to the immediate rather than the long-term effects of teaching.

**Evaluation of Degrees of Competence**

Evaluation for judging *relative* competence must take into account the probable multiple short- and long-run consequences of teaching behaviors and the substantive basis for teaching judgments. This type of evaluation depends on high-inference variables, e.g., how well does the teacher plan, within and across lessons, to impart the structure of knowledge in the discipline, to account for the students' levels of development and prior learning, and to achieve the immediate and long-range goals of instruction? How well do the teacher's strategies and techniques meet the changing needs of students over time, integrate different objectives, and foster the development, application, and transference of student skills and abilities? These high-inference variables require the judgment of an expert observer.

Three basic characteristics of an evaluation process designed to judge minimal competence may limit its validity for judging relative competence above a minimal level. These limitations stem from the expertise of the evaluator, the format of evaluation, and the evaluation criteria.

A generalist evaluator trained in evaluation techniques can ascertain the presence or absence of minimal teaching competencies in a few visits. Thus, principals can make defensible decisions about whether a teacher should or should not be placed on probationary status. Classroom management problems are difficult to hide, even on a prearranged observation day and even if students tend to behave better for their principal. Gross ineffectiveness in communication also is hard to disguise.

Under this method of evaluation, however, the principal, who is usually a generalist, cannot assess subject area competence and the quality of ongoing classroom activities. The kind of sophisticated, knowledge-based assessments required for valid ratings beyond satisfactory demands an expert in the teaching area of the evaluatee.

Furthermore, relative competence cannot be assessed solely on the basis of a few discrete classroom observations. The format of evaluation must reach beyond observed teaching behaviors on a given day or days. The quality of ongoing classroom activities depends on how what happens today relates to what happened yesterday and last week, as well as what will happen tomorrow and thereafter.

Because the internal coherence and integrity of teaching form a continuum, the evaluation of relative competence requires a more holistic set of data about teaching activities than can be gleaned from teacher performance during a few classroom observation visits. It requires a longitudinal assessment of teacher plans, classroom activities, and student performances and products.

Greenwich is distinguished by its emphasis on evaluating degrees of competence as it seeks to help teachers improve their performance. The validity of Greenwich's process rests on its ability to appropriately diagnose individual teacher's needs and to accurately gauge progress toward more competent performance in the areas so identified. Evaluation for improvement allows for individualized applications of teaching criteria, because teacher needs are personal to the teacher and individual to the classroom context. Thus, the Greenwich process has the capacity to help a teacher develop throughout his or her career.

Unlike processes for evaluating minimal competence, the Greenwich process continues to be relevant as the teacher acquires the ability to make professional judgments. Although the substitution of specialists for generalist evaluators would improve the process, mutual goal setting helps it to remain relevant for experienced teachers.

Some criteria represented in the Greenwich Guidelines for Professional Performance can even guide the judgment of excellence. The guidelines include such criteria as: "uses instructional techniques that are current, resourceful, and challenging"; "recognizes differences in capacities and interests of students"; "enriches the daily program through a variety of interests"; "shows understanding, interest, and concern for students' emotional, social, and physical characteristics"; "develops in students a respect for learning [and] a consideration of the rights, feelings, and ideas of others"; and "seeks to understand different sides of a question."

In designating teachers as outstanding in their year-end assessment reports, Greenwich principals ensure that these designations may be justifiably inferred from the evaluation reports. This documentation is intended to protect outstanding teachers from possible reductions in force. The validity of these judgments for this use has yet to be tested. The outcome will prove informative.

Given current public interest in diversifying the uses of teacher evaluation for personnel decisionmaking, we discuss below the potential validity of these processes for other types of personnel decisions. Indeed, all of these districts make differentiated staffing decisions when they select senior teachers, teacher leaders, consulting teachers, ITIP trainers, peer advisers, and so on. Yet none uses its teacher evaluation process for selecting these teachers. Why not?

These districts use committees of teachers and administrators to select differentiated staff on the basis of administrator and peer recommendations. In Toledo, for example, the Intern Review Panel selects consulting teachers who have been recommended for their teaching excellence, creativity in teaching, school leadership, self-confidence, ability to handle emergencies, ability to generate ideas and solutions, and human relations skills.

Peer advisers in Salt Lake City are nominated by principals and teachers and selected by a committee on the basis of their teaching ability, interpersonal skills, and discretion in dealing with peers, students, parents, and administrators. Senior teachers in Greenwich are self-nominated and selected by a committee of school-level administrators and teachers on the basis of their ability to express themselves and to motivate students, as well as their subject-matter knowledge.

Although the screening processes for these positions would likely eliminate teachers who had received poor evaluations, the evaluation processes would not provide recommendations for this special status. First, the evaluation processes do not produce the kinds of information about teaching competence that would be needed to differentiate between good, better, and outstanding teachers. But more important, the differentiated staff roles require a wider range of talents than those exhibited in the classroom.

In sum, the evaluation processes of these four districts do not suit the selection of differentiated staff. Thus, LEAs seeking innovative personnel policies must decide whether their goal is to reward teachers for classroom performance or to select teachers for leadership positions. The former requires assessing degrees of competence; the latter requires more.

## UTILITY

The utility of teacher evaluation depends in part on its reliability and validity, that is, on how consistently and accurately the process measures minimal competence and degrees of competence. The utility of evaluation depends also on its cost, that is, on whether it achieves usable outcomes without generating excessive costs. The results must be worth the time and effort used to obtain them if the process is to survive competing organizational demands. At least three types of costs—logistic, financial, and political—should be considered in assessing utility.

*Logistic costs*: Evaluation procedures, if overly complicated, threaten utility. A process too cumbersome to provide timely results loses its utility. If procedural demands exceed staff capabilities, evaluation is implemented poorly and its results are not usable because they are not reliable or valid. A process that is too complicated or too time-consuming to be properly implemented has low utility where teacher organizations can block dismissal attempts on procedural grounds. Equally important, excessively complicated procedures dilute evaluation resources, making them less available for improvement purposes.

*Financial costs*: As resources devoted to evaluation increase, so must the perceived, observable benefits of evaluation. If the financial costs of the process exceed its perceived benefits, utility suffers. Sooner or later, the system will commit less time and money to the process so as to accommodate other system demands, and the process will lose its utility. The evaluation process must be cost-effective enough to allow for a sustained level of effort over time.

*Political costs*: Useful evaluation requires political acceptability. A process may be theoretically valid and reliable, but if it is not endorsed by those who control political power, the use of its results will lead to struggles that divert organizational energies from system goals. Similarly, if the process undermines the ability of important constituents—teachers, parents, or administrators—to legitimately influence the teaching-learning environment, it will breed dissension or low morale that adversely affects the larger organizational mission.

Utility represents a proper balance of costs and benefits. The benefits include the provision of data for decisionmaking, better communication, and personnel improvement.

*Data for decisionmaking*: The evaluation process must produce data of sufficient quality and relevance that administrators, teachers, and others will use the information in making personnel and organizational decisions.

*Better communications*: The evaluation process should promote communication among members of the organization. To the extent that it provides opportunities for disseminating organizational goals, it will help to maintain and improve the organization.

*Personnel improvement*: To the extent that the evaluation process leads incompetent performers to depart and competent performers to improve, the quality of teaching and instruction will improve.

The design and implementation of teacher evaluation processes depend on these aspects of utility. However, they are rarely considered in the literature, which treats issues of reliability and validity in isolation from real-world complexities and constraints. Many theoretically and technically sound evaluation systems fail in their implementation because they do not take into account the logistic, financial, or political realities that ultimately determine their usefulness.

The evaluation processes in the four case study districts achieve higher utility than most, since their results are used, and the processes have proved cost-effective enough to remain viable (and relatively well implemented) over time. The components of utility, though, are not identical across districts or stable over time. As politics shift and the context and purposes of evaluation change, the utility of a given approach fluctuates also. Below we discuss the utility of the four districts' evaluation processes.

## Toledo

Judged in terms of its relatively narrow focus, Toledo's process has high utility. The intern and intervention programs succeed in assisting teachers to achieve acceptable teaching competence, or in removing them from the classroom if they do not. The process does both of these things without disrupting the system's operations or lowering the morale of school personnel.

Three critical features ensure the utility of the Toledo process: (1) It is carefully managed, and it is conducted by evaluators who have no other, competing responsibilities; (2) it is focused and it uses limited resources to reach a carefully defined subset of teachers; and (3) it is a collaborative effort and it engages the key political actors in the design, implementation, and ongoing redesign of the process.

By giving consulting teachers released time and limiting the number of interns each evaluates, the process provides more and closer supervision of teachers being evaluated and increases usefulness of evaluation for both individual interns and for decisionmakers. The process precludes the all-too-common type of evaluation characterized by last-minute observation or no observation at all, poor documentation, and missed deadlines.

By focusing the intern and intervention programs on two specific subsets of teachers needing special assistance, the process is cost-effective in a particular sense. Although the cost of supervising each intern or intervention teacher averaged about a relatively high $2000 per supervised teacher in the first two years of the program's implementation, the process showed a relatively low overall cost and provided substantial substantive and political benefits.

The process ensures that only competent teachers enter the profession and that incompetent teachers are rejected if they show no improvement. These are the basic aims of teacher evaluation. For the general public, as well as for the school system and the teaching profession, a process that achieves these two complementary objectives has high utility.

By targeting resources on teachers who most need supervision, the process provides a cost-effective means of facilitating the organization's work. Inchoate efforts to handle the problems caused by a small number of incompetent teachers cause institutional confusion and divert considerable professional resources from instruction. In such cases, the organization must deal with the results of the problem rather than its source, and school operations suffer.

In contrast, a system that intensely supervised all teachers would waste valuable resources on many who did not require assistance; these resources also could be used more profitably for actual instruction rather than the monitoring of instruction. For accountability purposes at least, the Toledo intern and intervention programs have high utility: They achieve their goals without diverting resources from other aspects of the organization's mission.

Finally, because the Toledo programs are a joint venture of union and management, the political climate for implementation is more positive than would otherwise be the case. A review board handles administrators' and teachers' concerns, and procedural mechanisms ensure carefully conducted, fair supervision. As a consequence, the results of the process and the process itself are not subject to continual grievances. If the district terminates a teacher's contract, the union does not initiate proceedings against the district (it will, however, represent a teacher who requests legal assistance). This positive political atmosphere contributes to the programs' utility.

The small size of the intervention program also contributes to the political acceptability of the process. While some might argue that a program involving so few teachers can have little effect on organizational improvement, others hold that a program of broader scope might threaten organizational stability and morale. Toledo has balanced accountability and improvement needs by providing other voluntary vehicles for assistance that are not linked to personnel decisions.

In sum, the intern-intervention approach has high utility because it effectively targets resources on a small but important aspect of teacher supervision. It does so with the full cooperation of union and management and with increasing acceptance and approval by school personnel.

**Salt Lake City**

Salt Lake City's remediation process also has fairly high utility for accountability purposes, although it seems to provoke more anxiety on the part of teachers than does Toledo's process. This anxiety may stem from the fact that the principal alone makes the decision to move a teacher from the informal accountability process into the remediation process, and he makes the decision on grounds that are not uniform and prespecified. Or, it may stem from the fact that a teacher may be identified as a possible candidate for remediation because of a "review of services" request initiated by anyone in the school community.

The relative lack of standardization in evaluation prior to remediation does not seem to have resulted in the assignment of the wrong teachers to remediation. Neither has it weakened the use of the remediation process for personnel decisions. Over a nine-year period, remediation resulted in the removal of 37 teachers from a force now numbering 1100. Nearly that number were successfully remediated.

The financial costs of the remediation process are fairly low, since it relies in large part on the services of people receiving modest stipends or substitute pay. A four-member remediation team observes, advises, and evaluates a teacher for a period of up to five months, but the team members also have full-time responsibilities elsewhere. An additional teacher, drawn from among retired teachers or teachers on leave, may be hired full-time for up to a month to help the teacher on remediation.

Furthermore, although teacher association leaders express some concern about the role conflicts inherent in the teacher evaluation system, they accept it in the context of shared governance in Salt Lake. Under shared governance, teachers are members of the remediation teams and participate in virtually every aspect of school operations. Teacher control over curriculum decisions and involvement in other teaching policy decisions indirectly enhance the utility of the teacher evaluation process by legitimizing its main purpose: to ensure that incompetent teachers are removed from the school system.

**Lake Washington**

The utility of Lake Washington's teacher evaluation process for identifying, assisting, and, if necessary, removing incompetent teachers from the classroom is fairly high. Over a five-year period, the probationary process has directly resulted in four teachers leaving classroom teaching and in seven teachers improving sufficiently to be reinstated in the classroom on continuing contracts. The overall evaluation process has facilitated the counseling out of an additional 56 teachers, the placement of 21 teachers on leave of absence, and the nonrenewal of nine expired contracts. Lake Washington teachers and administrators agree that the process works fairly to facilitate personnel decisionmaking related to minimal competence.

Despite Lake Washington's tough-minded approach to evaluation, the political costs have not yet proved unbearable. Most teachers consider the evaluators fair, equitable, and consistent. The ongoing training provided to administrators has minimized teacher perceptions of individual evaluator bias. Union representatives have said that "if an administrator uses the procedure correctly, we are not going to be against them."

The financial and logistic costs of this process are large. Of the four districts in the study, Lake Washington invests the greatest amount of resources in teacher evaluation, particularly because its staff development expenditures must be included. (Greenwich also makes a major investment in staff development, but its operation is separate from teacher evaluation.)

Lake Washington elementary school principals spend an average of 26 percent of their time on evaluation; secondary administrators spend some 15 percent. The staff development budget was increased to $1 million in 1983–1984. This allocation finances the ITIP program for the development of the instructional ability of teachers, other in-service training for teachers, individual teacher and school staff development, and administrator training in a variety of areas, including clinical supervision skills.

These expenditures of time and money produce visible benefits. The ITIP precepts that guide staff development for principals and teachers bring cohesiveness to an activity that is usually fragmented and erratic and helps teachers and their supervisors to identify and clarify problems. The ITIP framework also gives them tools and a common vantage point for developing pragmatic solutions. The investment in staff development thus increases the utility of teacher evaluation.

However, the highly specified, time-consuming, and cumbersome procedures for evaluation decrease its utility in two ways. First, the procedures discourage the use of probation in many instances where both teachers and administrators feel it is called for. Second, they leave little time for attention to the needs of competent teachers.

The probationary procedures prescribed by state law consume considerable time. District practices require additional time. Principals must continually assess teacher response to their personal growth plan, and they must observe and meet at least once a week with the probationary teacher. This enormous investment of time conforms to the district philosophy of doing everything possible to help a teacher improve.

The enormous investment of time also means that, regardless of the actual state of teaching in a school, principals believe that they can deal with no more than one teacher on probation at a time. A number of principals frankly admit that they are often forced to transfer ineffective teachers rather than to place them on probation. Lake Washington teachers also believe strongly and with surprising consistency that the system tolerates incompetent classroom performance.

The procedural requirements for teacher evaluation in Lake Washington, which emanate largely from the state law, prevent district administrators from devising a more productive evaluation strategy. District teachers and administrators believe that teacher evaluation requires differentiated practices to reflect teacher skill and needs. The utility of the evaluation process is reduced by the need to minimally evaluate all teachers for the same amount of time every year, as the state requires. This procedural uniformity results in pro forma evaluations in many cases and lack of special attention to excellence, and it prevents administrators from directing evaluation resources where they are most needed.

As the overall quality of teaching in Lake Washington has improved, the need for differentiated teacher evaluation has increased. The decreased utility of the current process stems in part from the rigidity of its procedures in the face of changing purposes and needs.

## Greenwich

The Greenwich teacher evaluation system requires that every teacher engage in goal setting, consultation, observation, and evaluation every year. To permit adequate time for teacher evaluation, teacher leaders are assigned to schools to maintain a ratio of about one evaluator to 20 evaluatees. We estimated that principals would have to spend 9 percent of their time to minimally meet the demands of the process. The time spent by principals, other building-level administrators (assistant principals, certain department chairpersons), and teacher leaders represents a major commitment of resources.

The major goal of the system is to improve teaching. Unlike the other three districts, where the departure of some incompetent teachers presumptively raises the quality of teaching, Greenwich cannot as easily quantify the effects of its system. Greenwich annually surveys its teachers about their perceptions of the fairness and utility of the teacher evaluation process. About half report that the system helps them improve their teaching performance. While reports of improved performance do not always mean improved performance, they may indicate feelings of efficacy that ultimately improve performance.[2]

The use of joint goal setting and teacher self-evaluation (along with administrator evaluation) increases the likelihood that teachers will find the process useful. Although many evaluation systems use goal-setting procedures, they do not always specifically address the teachers' own immediate concerns, classroom situations, and areas in which there is already a felt need for improvement.

The Greenwich system not only enables the school system to engage the individual teacher, it does so in a manner that relates directly (or at least should relate) to the teachers' daily professional endeavors. Thus, the utility of the Greenwich evaluation process results from its ability to tap teacher motivation and desire for self-improvement and to reward teachers' efforts by acknowledging their importance.

The ability of the evaluation process to provide this stimulus for improvement justifies its financial and logistic costs. However, to the extent that the process loses its relevance to many teachers, its expenditures of time and effort produce less and its utility diminishes. The current trend to replace teachers' personal goals with system goals may be having this effect.

The Greenwich teacher evaluation system is not designed to serve accountability purposes. However, Greenwich is currently trying to

---

[2]Other research suggests that teachers typically do not attribute positive effects on their teaching to teacher evaluation processes (see, e.g., Natriello and Dornbusch, 1980–1981).

standardize the process and the criteria for evaluation so that it can use the results of evaluation as a basis for individual personnel or job status decisions. Although we found little evidence that the process has been used for personnel decisions, many teachers and some administrators believe that its use for that purpose conflicts with its use for improvement. Teachers and some evaluators are selecting meaningful personal goals more cautiously, thus reducing the value of the system.

Politically, the Greenwich teacher evaluation process has cost little and provided few benefits. The process does not produce the kinds of tangible outcomes that have great meaning to the public. While the perceived benefits to the school system have sufficed to support additional resources for evaluation (primarily in the form of teacher leaders) over many years, the perceived utility of evaluation has not sufficed to protect evaluation time against other organizational demands. Both principals and teacher leaders complain that other administrative duties reduce the time available for teacher evaluation. In assigning teacher leaders other administrative functions, the Greenwich educational authorities appear to have somewhat devalued the evaluation function.

The political costs of the evaluation process may be expected to increase if and when results are used for personnel decisions. If the process is well enough adapted to this new purpose and resources are increased to meet reliability demands, the political benefits of the process may also increase. Teacher support for the evaluation system will depend upon how well it continues to fulfill its traditional purpose as well as its new objectives.

In sum, the utility of a teacher evaluation system depends on how well and how fairly it measures what it seeks to measure, whether the school system can and will tolerate its logistic and financial costs, and whether it functions so as to be acceptable to the relevant political forces. The utility of a given approach changes as the politics, context, and purposes of evaluation change.

Toledo will, in a few years, have to hire many more new teachers. With that, the cost of the intern program as currently implemented will rise substantially. Will the program survive? Will Salt Lake's unusual shared governance and nonstandardization survive without the current superintendent's leadership? Will Lake Washington, which has attained prominence through standardization, find that its procedures must give way to a differentiated evaluation strategy? How will Greenwich resolve its competing demands for professional growth and accountability?

The utility of a specific teacher evaluation approach will vary over time. School districts, we suggest in the final section, should proceed analytically.

# V. CONCLUSIONS AND RECOMMENDATIONS

We undertook this study to find teacher evaluation practices that produce information that school districts can use for helping teachers to improve and/or for making personnel decisions. We described in this report four evaluation procedures that achieve these primary objectives.

Our conclusions and recommendations constitute a set of necessary, but not sufficient, conditions for successful teacher evaluation. Educational policies and procedures must be tailored to local circumstances. Our conclusions and recommendations, therefore, may be best thought of as heuristics, or starting strategies to be modified on the basis of local experience.

> Conclusion One: *To succeed, a teacher evaluation system must suit the educational goals, management style, conception of teaching, and community values of the school district.*

As obvious as this conclusion may appear, the educational landscape is nevertheless littered with the remnants of unsuccessful procedures produced by bygone fads, administrators, and policies. The procedures failed—that is, lost their relevance and ceased to be faithfully implemented—in part because they did not serve the school system's more fundamental operating assumptions.

In each of the study districts, the teacher evaluation system worked as intended because it matched the fundamental operating assumptions of the district's educational goals, management style, conception of teaching, and community values. Where a district's ethos and operating assumptions were changing, we saw evidence of strain in the implementation of teacher evaluation.

This conclusion suggests that a school district that values uniformity of instruction and emphasizes standardized testing as the measure of goal attainment should not adopt a teacher evaluation process that allows multiple definitions of teaching success. A district that values multiple outcomes of teaching and learning should not use standardized test scores for evaluating teachers.

A highly centralized, bureaucratic district should probably not adopt a teacher evaluation process that allows individual teachers to set their own goals; a highly decentralized district should probably not use an evaluation process that stresses adherence to centrally determined goals and uniform curricular objectives. A district that wants teachers to take responsibility for their own professional development should probably use teachers as well as administrators as evaluators.

A district in which management values predominate probably cannot for long delegate evaluation responsibility to a teachers' association or to individual teachers. A district with a strong teachers' association probably cannot usefully use a traditional hierarchical approach to evaluation.

Based on the conclusion that a teacher evaluation system is more likely to succeed if it suits a district's fundamental operating assumptions, we recommend:

1. The school district should examine its educational goals, management style, conception of teaching, and community values and adopt a teacher evaluation system compatible with them. It should not adopt an evaluation system simply because that system works in another district.
2. States should not impose highly prescriptive teacher evaluation requirements.

Conclusion Two: *Top-level commitment to and resources for evaluation outweigh checklists and procedures.*

This simple conclusion may be the most important of the study. Successful teacher evaluation demands commitment and resources. The top leader of the school administration and/or the teachers' organization must commit themselves to evaluation, and the school district must translate their commitment into resources. Without commitment and resources and the activities that they stimulate, teacher evaluation becomes a formal, meaningless exercise.

Some educators believe that good teacher evaluation requires no more than finding the right checklist. They collect and compare forms and choose one. Then they discuss such relatively minor details as whether the evaluator must spend an entire class period observing or whether the teacher should have advance notice.

We found that the form and procedure of the relatively few successful teacher evaluation systems vary little from those of the less successful systems. The successful ones are, however, distinguished by their seriousness of purpose and intensity of implementation. Many school districts evaluate teachers solely to comply with state law or regulation; others, solely to respond to community sentiment. Under these circumstances—which are more prevalent than most will admit—evaluation requires nothing more than formal compliance and minimal resource commitment. This approach cannot produce successful teacher evaluation, because it does not integrate evaluation into decisionmaking or give it priority.

Since evaluation is both a difficult and inherently uncomfortable activity, it needs explicit mechanisms to make it important—that is, to ensure that it receives high priority. Without such mechanisms, evaluators tend to put it aside for more immediate, and perhaps less onerous, demands on their time. When evaluation is not given priority, its quality and intensity are reduced and its results cannot be used for personnel decisionmaking or improvement purposes.

For school districts to obtain the commitment and resources needed to make evaluation important and useful, we recommend:

> 3. The school district should give evaluators sufficient time, unencumbered by competing administrative demands, for evaluation. This may mean assigning staff other than the school principal to some evaluation functions.

Time is the main resource for teacher evaluation. Evaluators need time to make reliable and valid judgments and to offer assistance. Administrators and teachers who evaluate other teachers must not have urgent competing responsibilities that take precedence over evaluation.

The school district must create an incentive structure that encourages and allows evaluators to evaluate thoroughly. That is, having mandated teacher evaluation, the district must provide time for evaluation. It must create time either by giving evaluation a higher priority than that of competing responsibilities or by assigning additional evaluators. All of our case study districts solved this problem by assigning expert teachers to some aspect of the evaluation process, particularly to providing more intensive supervision to teachers most needing assistance.

Having allocated the time, the district must take steps to ensure that evaluators use the time well. For this purpose, we recommend:

> 4. The school district should regularly assess the quality of evaluation, including individual and collective evaluator competence. The assessments should provide feedback to individual evaluators and input into the continuing evaluator training process.

The district must review evaluations both to increase their reliability and to ensure their timeliness. The evaluation of teachers with whom the evaluators must continue to work may create conflict. Evaluators, particularly principals, face competing considerations: On the one hand, they may want to overrate teachers so as to preserve harmonious working relations in the school. On the other hand, they may want to deal with the unpleasantness associated with teacher evaluation by deferring evaluation.

The district must therefore reinforce evaluators to conduct reliable, valid, and timely reviews as part of its strategy for creating a proper incentive structure. Reinforcement may take the form of evaluating principals (and other evaluators) on the basis of how well they evaluate teachers, creating a central office position or committee to oversee evaluation reporting, and/or developing a formal mechanism for monitoring and periodically revising the evaluation process.

Because teacher evaluation is a judgmental rather than a scientific process, it must be conducted fairly. This means that evaluators must share a common understanding of the process, its implementation, and the assumptions on which its reliability and validity rest. Moreover, as time passes, the actual implementation of the evaluation process may change as experience grows. Thus, the nature and quality of implementation must be monitored. Evaluators need regular, periodic opportunities to share their understanding of the purpose and process. Therefore, we recommend:

    5. The school district should train evaluators in observation and evaluation techniques, including reporting, diagnosis, and clinical supervision skills, when it adopts a new teacher evaluation process.

Furthermore, a shared understanding of the criteria on which judgments of teaching are made must be developed and maintained by providing continuing opportunities for evaluators to discuss the teaching assumptions underlying evaluation criteria and to review actual evaluations with each other and their superiors. The content of evaluator training (and, indeed, the choice of evaluators) must suit the major purposes of evaluation.

Although we consider checklists and procedures less important than commitment and resources, we nevertheless advise districts to pay attention to them. These technical details focus discussion. In the process of agreeing on evaluation form and substance, evaluators develop a mutual understanding about teaching in their district and a common language of analysis and interpretation. Evaluation provides one opportunity to establish and communicate a philosophy of teaching. This philosophy may involve not only training, administrative leadership, and resource allocation, but also the details of what makes good teaching.

Conclusion Three: *The school district must decide the main purpose of its teacher evaluation system and then match the process to the purpose.*

Teacher evaluation serves multiple purposes, and a school district may be tempted to try to serve all of its purposes with one set of evaluators, using a single instrument and a single process. Furthermore, a district may not want, for political reasons, to say that its goal is helping all teachers to improve if this means that it will appear to be rejecting the elimination of incompetents as its main purpose. Conversely, if its main purpose is eliminating incompetents, it would not want to seemingly reject helping all teachers to improve. Many districts, therefore, publicly proclaim that they are addressing all concerns.

With the new interest in merit pay and master teachers, we may assume that many school districts will try to use one evaluation system for both traditional and these new purposes. Yet, most of the literature questions whether a single evaluation system can handle both formative (improvement-oriented) and summative (decision-oriented) evaluation. It suggests that decision-oriented evaluation would intimidate rather than help teachers and that improvement-oriented evaluation produces data unsuited to personnel decisions. This explanation, while correct as far as it goes, fails to fully explain the dynamics.

Our case studies reinforce the conclusion that a single teacher evaluation process can serve only one goal well. Sometimes an aspect of a process can serve both decisionmaking and improvement purposes for a small subset of teachers (e.g., in a remediation program); however, a single process cannot meet the goals of judging and improving *all* teachers. The reasons for this become clear when we examine the demands associated with several evaluation purposes.

Evaluation for improvement, if it is to meet the needs of all teachers, must be flexible, for, like individualized instruction, it must take each teacher where he or she is and help him or her improve. It must encourage teachers to develop. Criteria must be broad enough and rating scales must have sufficient range to accommodate all.

To be helpful to the teacher, the evaluation process must take into account the specific teaching context. The outcome of the process is advice to the teacher. It is not important, indeed it is not necessary, possible, or realistic, for school administrators to expect to be able to *compare* teachers under this type of evaluation. The flexibility needed to provide useful personalized advice to a teacher precludes comparisons or rankings of teachers. If the purpose were narrowed to helping only those who are judged to need it, the process would begin to acquire some of the characteristics associated with other purposes which, because they compare teachers, require a higher order of reliability and a different kind of validity.

Evaluation for the possible termination of employment has different requirements. The criteria and the ratings must be designed to allow decisions about minimally acceptable teaching behaviors. The evaluation task is to distinguish competent from incompetent teachers. The basis for this distinction must be clear. Hence, the school district must specify the criteria, behavioral bases for ratings, and procedures. The bureaucratic demand is for a common scale on which all teachers may theoretically be compared, but the real need is for a list of teaching behaviors that all teachers except the incompetent will exhibit. In practice, this means that judgments typically rest on assessment of generic teaching skills.

The use of generic teaching skills as the basis for evaluation implies that the evaluator need not know much about the subject matter and grade-level pedagogical demands. Thus, a generalist principal can evaluate all teachers under his or her jurisdiction. Presumptive fairness means that the principal can observe all teachers for relatively short periods of time, noting that most teachers have the minimal skills but that the incompetent do not. Having made this determination, the principal (or district administration) may then concentrate evaluation resources on those who may be judged incompetent.

To spend substantial evaluation resources on all teachers in this approach would be wasteful since, by virtue of the focus on minimum skills (skills that, by definition, most teachers have), the process is irrelevant to the needs of most teachers. The school district can concentrate evaluation resources on helping the probationary teacher to master the minimum skills or, if this help fails, on making the final judgment of incompetence. It can offer personalized assistance using context-specific applications of the teaching criteria for improvement or remediation.

The final determination of incompetence, however, must be seen to be reliable. The probationary teacher must be judged by standardized indicators. Multiple samples of the teacher's behavior must be taken. In sum, the judgment must be reliable enough to stand up in a court of law, where a termination decision might be appealed.

Improvement and termination pose different evaluation demands. They require trade-offs between breadth and depth of coverage and between standardized and context-specific notions of acceptable, good, and better teaching. Bureaucratic and external public demands differ. The failure to clarify the purpose, or to match the process to the purpose, may undo the effectiveness of a teacher evaluation system. The case study districts explicitly or implicitly made their choices. If a school district wants to serve more than one purpose, it may need to establish more than one process. We recommend:

6. The school district should examine its existing teacher evaluation system to see which, if any, purpose it serves well. If the district changes the purpose, it should change the process.
7. The school district should decide whether it can afford more than one teacher evaluation process or whether it must choose a single process to fit its main purpose.

Although our study was restricted to school districts that used teacher evaluation for individual improvement and personnel decisions, we believe that some of what we learned applies to teacher evaluation for other purposes, such as decisions regarding merit pay or master teachers. Decisions that involve pay and promotion and *publicly* differentiate among teachers usually receive a high level of scrutiny and therefore require procedures that all parties perceive as reliable and valid.

The award of merit pay, while not as serious as a dismissal decision, nevertheless has visible consequences: It will label some teachers meritorious and others, by default, unmeritorious. The latter group will then want to scrutinize the process, especially when every teacher is evaluated every year.[1] Thus, the award of merit pay establishes the need for rigor in teacher evaluation to sustain the credibility of the process—a rigor that approaches the level required for dismissal decisions. A school district that intends to evaluate all teachers annually for merit pay decisions must commit substantial resources to evaluation.

Teacher evaluation to sustain master teacher appointments requires a somewhat smaller commitment of resources than that for merit pay. The evaluation process still demands rigor, but it will affect a smaller percentage of teachers in any given year. Thus, the school system will be able to concentrate its evaluation resources.

If the school district intends to consider most teachers for either merit pay or master teacher status (after a few years of experience), the evaluation system may resemble the system for termination; it need identify only those few to be denied merit pay or promotion. However, if only a fraction of teachers are to receive merit pay or master teacher status, the demands for reliability, validity, and public defensibility increase significantly.

---

[1] Some might argue that the award of merit pay could or should be kept confidential. Such a policy does not seem likely in the freedom-of-information era.

Evaluation for termination must reliably distinguish between inadequate and minimally adequate teachers; evaluation for excellence must reliably distinguish between marginally excellent and merely highly competent teachers. However, whereas a standard list suffices to distinguish low levels of competence, distinguishing among high levels of competence requires multiple criteria, expertly evaluated.

Excellent teaching is, by definition, rare; it is distinguished by judgment, intuition, insight, creativity, improvisations, and expressiveness. While criteria and scales can be devised to measure these intentional behaviors, evaluating their presence requires reliability; unreliable results are likely to be challenged.

The evaluation of excellent teaching, we believe, requires judgments by experts rather than by generalists. Whereas principals can evaluate for performance improvement (where the need for reliability is relatively low) and can evaluate for termination decisions (where the criteria are the least common denominators of teaching), the judgment of excellence requires an expert. Excellent teaching, we submit, cannot be judged in the abstract as is generic teaching competence. To judge excellence, an evaluator must know the subject-matter, grade-level, and teaching context of the teacher being evaluated.

In other words, skilled mathematics teachers are needed to judge excellence in mathematics teaching. Skilled elementary school teachers are needed to judge excellence in elementary teaching, and so on. Moreover, the evaluation of excellence calls for multiple samples of the teacher's behavior either by the same expert or by several experts. The dual requirements of expertness and reliability demand a teacher evaluation process based on either peer (or, more likely, master teacher) review or review by subject-matter supervisors.

> Conclusion Four: *To sustain resource commitments and political support, teacher evaluation must be seen to have utility. Utility depends on the efficient use of resources to achieve reliability, validity, and cost-effectiveness.*

For a teacher evaluation system to be useful to the district and credible to teachers, administrators, and the community, it should offer a plausible solution to the major perceived problems or needs of the teaching force. We saw in the case study districts that all participants supported (or at least accepted) the teacher evaluation systems. For a system to take hold and last, it must earn and retain the support of all participants. All participants are more likely to support a system that meets their needs.

The selection of a teacher evaluation system depends in part on the composition of the existing and anticipated teaching force. A district that will not be hiring for a decade needs an evaluation process that suits an experienced staff. A district with increasing enrollments or a teaching force rapidly approaching retirement may need an evaluation process that will improve hiring. A contracting district may need to consider performance-based reductions in force. A district with an even distribution of age and experience might choose an evaluation system that differs from one that might be used where age and experience are clustered.

The selection of a teacher evaluation system depends to an even greater extent on the perceived quality of the teaching force. The composition of the teaching force and perceptions of its quality determine which problems and needs the district should try to solve by teacher evaluation: general improvement, improvement of certain categories of teachers, identification of incompetence, assessment of relative competence, induction of new teachers, retention of more experienced teachers, rewarding outstanding performance, or selection of master teachers. If the district chooses a teacher evaluation system that addresses its needs, all involved are more likely to consider the evaluation system worthwhile.

The utility of teacher evaluation is difficult to assess. School districts do not keep their books so as to permit the calculation of the true cost of teacher evaluation. While some school districts earmark funds for teacher evaluation or staff development, these funds do not usually cover the cost associated with the time of those involved in the evaluation process.

The effects of teacher evaluation may be assessed in terms of, say, the cost of terminating an ineffective teacher's appointment or the percentage of teachers dismissed because of poor teaching. But, some of the most important effects may be indirect. Does the community believe that the school district is doing something about incompetent teachers and teaching? Does the school district have a mechanism for communicating its expectations to teachers? Are good teachers being recognized and reinforced? The answers to these and other questions may contribute to perceptions of the utility of a teacher evaluation system.

In the end, a school district considering whether to adopt a particular teacher evaluation system (or whether to eliminate one) must assess whether it is worth the cost. Do the results justify the human resources invested in it? The answer to this question depends on administrators', teachers', and the public's perception of the quality of the teaching force and the contribution that the teacher evaluation process makes to teaching quality. While the perception of each group to some extent reflects the group's interest, all are more likely to share a common perception of utility if the process achieves what it sets out to achieve. To increase the likelihood of perceived utility, we recommend:

>    8. The school district must allocate resources commensurate with the number of teachers to be evaluated and the importance and visibility of evaluation outcomes.

This recommendation extends our third recommendation: that districts should provide sufficient time for evaluation. Despite the obviousness of both propositions, most school districts fail to provide resources commensurate with the scope of their evaluations. The results therefore lack reliability, validity, and utility.

Many school systems review all teachers annually. Two bureaucratic phenomena encourage universal annual review. First, bureaucracies, especially public ones, must at least appear to treat all employees (and clients) alike. If a school district wants to evaluate some teachers, then it must evaluate all teachers so as not to discriminate. Second, teachers' associations want to prevent school administrators from singling out individual teachers for punitive evaluation. Hence, they often insist, through the collective bargaining process, that all teachers be evaluated annually.

The annual review of all teachers usually produces perfunctory evaluations, because evaluation resources (chiefly, the time of the principals and other evaluators) have been diluted to meet the formal requirement. Since many participants do not believe that the requirement leads to decisions, they do not press school systems to invest sufficiently in the process. The circular result is superficial evaluation that is not considered sufficiently reliable and valid to be used.

When pressed to improve teacher evaluation practices, school districts typically do not increase the ratio of evaluators to teachers but instead exhort principals to improve and increase evaluations. The supposedly enhanced process, while possibly occupying more time, still does not produce usable results.

Resource requirements depend also on the outcome sought. Results that decisively affect individual teachers demand a more thorough and reliable evaluation system than those that do not. Evaluation to help teachers to improve their performance, while important to teachers, does not affect them decisively. But evaluation used to terminate teachers' employment (or to make other teaching status decisions) has decisive effects.

As we have seen, the dismissal of a teacher requires multiple observations, extensive documentation, significant help to improve the teacher's performance, review of the decision at several levels, and due process. The school district must be prepared to legally defend the dismissal decision. Our next recommendation follows from these onerous resource requirements:

9. The school district should target resources so as to achieve real benefits.

Resources must go to the main evaluation purpose so that evaluation will be seen as cost-effective. The failure to concentrate resources will result in unfocused evaluation that consumes resources but produces information that serves neither teachers nor administrators.

When evaluation may lead to dismissal, for example, the school district must consolidate resources to provide multiple evaluations, that is, one evaluator making multiple observations (for accuracy); multiple evaluators making one or two observations (for fairness); or multiple evaluators making multiple observations (for accuracy and fairness). The failure to achieve accuracy and fairness will destroy the effectiveness of the teacher evaluation system. When costs are perceived to outweigh benefits, the process fails.

*Conclusion Five: Teacher involvement and responsibility improve the quality of teacher evaluation.*

The problems inherent in assigning the teacher evaluation function solely to principals came to our attention early in the study as we reviewed the literature and conducted our preliminary survey of school districts. Principals have a wide span of control and little time for evaluation, and they often experience conflicts as they try to balance their roles as school leader, supervisor, and builder of esprit de corps. Furthermore, they do not have specialized subject-matter or pedagogical knowledge of all teaching areas in which they are expected to evaluate teachers. These limitations on the principal as an evaluator of teachers often seriously impair the effectiveness of teacher evaluation processes.

All four of our case study districts use master teachers in some aspect of the evaluation process (and in other staff development activities as well). Although we did not select these districts for case study specifically because they involved highly qualified teachers in evaluation, we are convinced that the use of peer review and/or peer assistance greatly strengthens these districts' capacity to supervise teachers effectively by providing additional time and expertise for this function.

In addition, the teachers serving in various differentiated staff roles give their peers the kind of leadership and assistance that promotes the development and dissemination of professional standards of practice. In each district, expert teachers provide curricular advice, classroom assistance, and supervision both inside and outside the teacher evaluation process. Individually and collectively, teachers in these districts play a more nearly professional role than they do in districts that supervise and direct teachers through bureaucratic channels.

The involvement of the teachers' organization in the development and oversight of teacher evaluation—and of other teaching policies—also increases the effectiveness of an evaluation process. Particularly in districts where collective bargaining has contributed to the working conditions and the nature of the teaching force, union participation in designing and implementing evaluation is a virtual prerequisite for the acceptance of evaluation results.

When developing a teacher evaluation plan, a school district must consider issues of legitimacy and protection in their political context. More important, the *implementation* of teacher evaluation is itself a political process in which questions of credibility, due process, and fairness continually emerge in different forms. Collaboration between teachers and administrators in overseeing the implementation of evaluation can make the difference between useful evaluation results and stalemates.

In all of our case study districts, the teachers' organizations have played an important role in the design and implementation of the evaluation process. Their participation takes various forms, such as involvement in joint oversight committees, union appointment of teachers who assist in the evaluation process, and consultation between top administration officials and union leaders. As a result, the evaluation processes have enough legitimacy to produce usable results. Rather than seeking to constrain administrators' exercise of their authority through procedural requirements, organized teachers in these districts participate, in varying degrees, in the decisions that affect teachers *before* these decisions result in grievances.

Because the validity and utility of teacher evaluation depend so profoundly on who conducts and oversees evaluations, we recommend that:

10. The school district should involve expert teachers in the supervision and assistance of their peers, particularly beginning teachers and those in need of special assistance.

The use of expert teachers is probably the only practical way to give specialized help to teachers who need it. Expert teachers should be selected on the basis of their competence as teachers and their ability to provide supervision and assistance to adults. These experts should work only in their own teaching area to ensure informed and relevant help.

Expert teachers may be given released time (and/or additional contract time). Such time must be allocated for supervision and assistance and protected from other administrative duties. Of course, released time will increase costs and cause scheduling problems, particularly at the elementary school level. The added costs (primarily associated with additional or substitute teachers) provide time for supervision and assistance. The scheduling problem, while not trivial, is soluble; districts must experiment with new scheduling patterns.

11. The school district should involve teacher organizations in the design and oversight of teacher evaluation to ensure its legitimacy, fairness, and effectiveness.

The evaluation roles of management and teachers' organizations in districts where teachers participate in decisionmaking differ from their roles in districts that use traditional hierarchical evaluation practices. The traditional management role of enforcing accountability is typically seen as counterposing the traditional union role of affording protections. Teacher participation in evaluation obscures the distinctions between management prerogatives and teachers' rights. When teachers define and enforce professional standards of practice, they significantly reshape the traditional roles of both management and labor.

The shift from an adversarial to a participatory approach increases teachers' rights but also their responsibilities. It forces administrators to share power but gives them more freedom and legitimized authority to implement decisions once they are jointly made. This change accords teachers power over a greater range of educational matters at the cost of absolute protections based on work rules. Some may see this evolution toward professionalism as a threat to the basis of collective bargaining. Others may view it as a more mature stage of educational labor relations.

Districts that have reached a higher stage in labor relations can begin to redefine traditional management and labor roles (Mitchell and Kerchner, 1983, p. 220). This stage arrives only after the teachers' organization has amassed sufficient power to be accepted as a partner in policymaking. When this occurs, teacher professionalism in the modern context may not threaten unionism. In such districts as Toledo, where organized teachers participate in the definition of teaching and in decisions about membership in the profession, our study found the evolution of yet a higher stage in labor relations that goes beyond negotiated policy to *negotiated responsibility* as the basis for school district operations.

Negotiated responsibility provides the basis for a collective professionalism more potent than the individual professionalism that existed when unorganized teachers had only permissive authority over the substance of their work. It opens the way to collaborative control over teacher quality and creates a framework within which educators—teachers and administrators—can work together to improve the quality of their common professional work.

Teachers analyze the needs of their students, assess available resources, take cognizance of the school system's goals, and decide their instructional strategies. As they instruct, they modify their strategies to ensure that their instruction meets the needs of their students. They use a variety of means to assess whether the students have learned.

School districts evaluate teachers to ensure that teachers employ appropriate standards of practice. The conclusions and recommendations offered here are intended to lead to conditions that will help to improve the quality of teachers and teaching.

In the bureaucratic, or traditional, conception of teacher evaluation, the principal or another hierarchical superior of the teacher directly inspects the work of the teacher, i.e., observes the teacher engaged in the act of teaching. The principal typically assesses the observed behavior against a list of criteria furnished by the central administration. These criteria assume that teaching is planned, stable, and predictable. The principal then rates the teacher.

The professional conception involves master teachers in the evaluation of other teachers. The master teacher helps to enforce a professional standard of teaching. In this approach, the evaluator judges the *appropriateness* of teaching decisions. It assumes that teachers know subject matter and child development sufficiently well to make appropriate decisions for different students and classes.

Rather than attempting to force a consensus on a single proper standard of practice, the professional approach operates on a consensus of what is improper or inappropriate practice. In the absence of agreement on the one best system of instruction, master teachers sanction different standards of practice. Different circumstances and different teachers' personalities may lend themselves to different methods of instruction. But under no circumstances does the approach tolerate inappropriate educational practice.

Quality control through the enforcement of a professional standard of practice differs from quality control through prescribed curriculum and standardized testing. Both approaches contain risk. Bureaucratic policymaking makes teaching less attractive, thus lowering the quality of the teaching force which, in turn, causes districts to become more prescriptive in a vain effort to improve education.

The professional approach relies on people and judgments. It places more weight on the development of client-responsive practices than on the definition of standardized practice. It weeds out those unable or unwilling to develop competence, rather than controlling their damage by prescriptions for performance. It assumes that others will become more capable by engaging in the joint construction of goals, definition of standards of good practice, mutual criticism, and commitment to ongoing inquiry. It supposes that investing in staff development, career incentives, and evaluation, i.e., in teachers themselves, will improve the quality of teaching.

The bureaucratic approach has heavy costs; the time has come to try the professional approach to evaluation. We recommend, therefore:

12. The school district should hold teachers accountable to standards of practice that compel them to make appropriate instructional decisions on behalf of their students.

# REFERENCES

Anderson, B. D., "School Bureaucratization and Alienation from High School," *Sociology of Education* 46(2), 1973, 315–334.

Bandura, A., "Self-Efficacy Mechanism in Human Agency," *American Psychologist* 37(2), 1982, 122–147.

Bandura, A., and D. H. Schunk, "Cultivating Competence, Self-Efficacy, and Intrinsic Interest through Proximal Self-Motivation," *Journal of Personality and Social Psychology* 41, 1981, 586–598.

Bandura, A., et al., "Tests of the Generality of Self-Efficacy Theory," *Cognitive Therapy and Research* 4, 1980, 39–66.

Berman, P., and M. W. McLaughlin, *Federal Programs Supporting Educational Change*, The Rand Corporation, R-1589-HEW, 1978.

Bodine, R., "Teachers' Self-Assessment," in E. R. House (ed.), *School Evaluation*, McCutchan, Berkeley, Calif., 1973.

Brophy, J. E., and C. Evertson, *Process-Product Correlations in the Texas Teacher Effectiveness Study: Final Report*, Research and Development Center for Teacher Education, University of Texas, Austin, 1974.

Broudy, H. S., "Craft or Profession?" *The Educational Forum*, January 1956, 175–184.

Bushman, J. H., "Are Teachers Playing 'Statue' in the Classroom?" *NASSP Bulletin* 58, 1974, 386.

Coker, H., D. Medley, and R. Soar, "How Valid Are Expert Opinions about Effective Teaching?" *Phi Delta Kappan* 62(2), 1980, 131–134, 149.

Cronbach, L. J., "Beyond the Two Disciplines of Scientific Psychology," *American Psychologist* 30, 1975, 116–127.

Cronbach, L. J., and R. E. Snow, *Aptitudes and Instructional Methods: A Handbook for Research on Interactions*, Irvington, New York, 1977.

Darling-Hammond, Linda, Arthur E. Wise, and Sara R. Pease, "Teacher Evaluation in the Organizational Context: A Review of the Literature," *Review of Educational Research*, Fall 1983.

DiClemente, C. C., "Self-Efficacy and Smoking Cessation Maintenance: A Preliminary Report," *Cognitive Therapy and Research* 5, 1981, 175–187.

Doyle, W., "Paradigms for Research on Teacher Effectiveness," in L. S. Shulman (ed.), *Review of Research in Education*, Vol. 5, F. E. Peacock, Itasca, Illinois, 1978.

Dunkin, M. J., and B. J. Biddle, *The Study of Teaching*, Holt, Rinehart and Winston, New York, 1974.

Eisner, E. W., "On the Uses of Educational Connoisseurship and Criticism for Evaluating Classroom Life," *Teachers College Record* 78, 1978, 345–358.

Fenstermacher, G. D., and D. C. Berliner, *A Conceptual Framework for the Analysis of Staff Development*, The Rand Corporation, N-2046-NIE, 1983.

Fenstermacher, G. D., "A Philosophical Consideration of Recent Research on Teacher Effectiveness," in L. S. Shulman (ed.), *Review of Research in Education*, Vol. 6, F. E. Peacock, Itasca, Illinois, 1978.

Fuller, B., et al., "The Organizational Context of Individual Efficacy," *Review of Educational Research* 52(1), 1982, 7–30.

Gage, N. L., *The Scientific Basis of the Art of Teaching*, Teachers College Press, New York, 1978.

Knapp, M. S., *Toward the Study of Teacher Evaluation as an Organizational Process: A Review of Current Research and Practice*, Educational and Human Services Research Center, SRI International, Menlo Park, Calif., 1982.

Lewin, K., *The Conceptual Representation and the Measurement of Psychological Forces*, Duke University Press, Durham, North Carolina, 1938.

Lewin, K., T. Dembo, L. Festinger, and P. Sears, "Level of Aspiration," in J. Hunt (ed.), *Personality and Behavioral Disorders*, Vol. 2, Ronald Press, New York, 1944.

Mann, D. (ed.), *Making Change Happen?* Teachers College Press, New York, 1978.

McDonald, F. J., and P. Elias, *Executive Summary Report: Beginning Teacher Evaluation Study, Phase II*, Educational Testing Service, Princeton, New Jersey, 1976.

McKeachie, W. J., and J. A. Kulik, "Effective College Teaching," in F. N. Kerlinger (ed.), *Review of Research in Education*, Vol. 3, F. E. Peacock, Itasca, Illinois, 1975.

McNeil, J., and W. Popham, "The Assessment of Teacher Competence," in R. M. Travers (ed.), *Second Handbook of Research on Teaching*, Rand McNally, Chicago, 1973.

Medley, D. M., "The Effectiveness of Teachers," in P. L. Peterson and H. J. Walberg (eds.), *Research on Teaching*, McCutchan, Berkeley, Calif., 1979.

Millman, J. (ed.), *Handbook of Teacher Evaluation*, Sage Publications, Beverly Hills, Calif., 1981.

Mitchell, D. E., and C. T. Kerchner, "Collective Bargaining and Teacher Policy," in L. S. Shulman and G. Sykes (eds.), *Handbook of Teaching and Policy*, Longman, New York, 1983.

National Education Association, *Teacher Opinion Poll*, Washington, D.C., 1979.

Natriello, G., and S. M. Dornbusch, "Pitfalls in the Evaluation of Teachers by Principals," *Administrator's Notebook* 29(6), 1980–1981, entire issue.

Ouchi, W. G., "Markets, Bureaucracies, and Clans," *Administrative Science Quarterly* 25(1), 1980, 129–141.

Peterson, K., and D. Kauchak, *Teacher Evaluation: Perspectives, Practices and Promises*, Center for Educational Practice, University of Utah, Salt Lake City, 1982.

Peterson, P. L., "Interactive Effects of Student Anxiety, Achievement Orientation, and Teacher Behavior on Student Achievement and Attitude," unpublished doctoral dissertation, Stanford University, 1976.

Peterson, P. L., "Direct Instruction Reconsidered," in P. L. Peterson and H. J. Walberg (eds.), *Research on Teaching*, McCutchan, Berkeley, Calif., 1979.

Pfeffer, J., G. Salancik, and H. Leblebici, "The Effect of Uncertainty on the Use of Social Influence in Organizational Decision Making," *Administrative Science Quarterly* 21(2), 1976, 227–248.

Riley, R. D., and E. C. Schaffer, "Self-Certification: Accounting to Oneself," *Journal of Teacher Education* 30(2), 1979, 23–26.

Rosenholtz, S. J., and B. Wilson, "The Effect of Classroom Structure on Shared Perceptions of Ability," *American Educational Research Journal* 17, 1980, 75–82.

Rosenshine, B., and N. Furst, "Research on Teacher Performance Criteria," in B. O. Smith (ed.), *Research in Teacher Education: A Symposium*, Prentice-Hall, Englewood Cliffs, New Jersey, 1971.

Sabatier, P., and D. Mazmanian, *The Implementation of Regulatory Policy: A Framework of Analysis*, Institute of Governmental Affairs, Davis, Calif., 1979.

Shavelson, R., "What Is *the* Basic Teaching Skill?" *Journal of Teacher Education* 14, 1973, 144–151.

Shavelson, R., and N. Dempsey-Atwood, "Generalizability of Measures of Teacher Behavior," *Review of Educational Research* 46, 1976, 553–612.

Shavelson, R., and P. Stern, "Research on Teachers' Pedagogical Thoughts, Judgments, Decisions and Behavior," *Review of Educational Research* 51(4), 1981, 455–498.

Soar, R. S., *Follow Through Classroom Process Measurement and Pupil Growth*, Institute for Development of Human Resources, University of Florida, Gainesville, 1972.

Soar, R. S., "An Integration of Findings from Four Studies of Teacher Effectiveness," in G. D. Borich (ed.), *The Appraisal of Teaching: Concepts and Process*, Addison-Wesley, Reading, Mass., 1977.

Soar, R. S., and R. M. Soar, "An Attempt to Identify Measures of Teacher Effectiveness from Four Studies," *Journal of Teacher Education* 27, 1976, 261–267.

Sproull, L. S., *Response to Regulation: An Organizational Process Framework*, Carnegie-Mellon University, Pittsburgh, Penna., 1979.

Stallings, J. A., "How Instructional Processes Relate to Child Outcomes," in G. D. Borich (ed.), *The Appraisal of Teaching: Concepts and Process*, Addison-Wesley, Reading, Mass., 1977.

Talbert, J., *School Organization and Institutional Changes: Exchange and Power in Loosely Coupled Systems*, Institute for Research on Educational Finance and Governance, Stanford University, Stanford, Calif., 1980.

Weatherley, R., and M. Lipsky, "Street-Level Bureaucrats and Institutional Innovation: Implementing Special Education Reform," *Harvard Educational Review* 47(2), 1977, 171–197.

Wildavsky, A., *Speaking Truth to Power: The Art and Craft of Policy Analysis*, Little, Brown and Company, Boston, 1980.

# THE CHICAGO PUBLIC LIBRARY

## FOR REFERENCE USE ONLY
Not to be taken from this building

**SOCIAL SCIENCES & HISTORY DIVISION**

RAND/R-3139-NIE